Coconuts and Collards

UNIVERSITY PRESS OF FLORIDA

Florida A&M University, Tallahassee
Florida Atlantic University, Boca Raton
Florida Gulf Coast University, Ft. Myers
Florida International University, Miami
Florida State University, Tallahassee
New College of Florida, Sarasota
University of Central Florida, Orlando
University of Florida, Gainesville
University of North Florida, Jacksonville
University of South Florida, Tampa
University of West Florida, Pensacola

Coconuts & Collards

Recipes and Stories from Puerto Rico to the Deep South

Von Diaz

Photographs by Cybelle Codish

University Press of Florida

Gainesville · Tallahassee · Tampa · Boca Raton

Pensacola · Orlando · Miami · Jacksonville · Ft. Myers · Sarasota

Copyright 2018 by Von Diaz
Printed in Korea on acid-free paper

23 22 21 20 19 18   6 5 4 3 2 1

Library of Congress Control Number: 2017947181
ISBN 978-0-8130-5665-4

The University Press of Florida is the scholarly
publishing agency for the State University System
of Florida, comprising Florida A&M University,
Florida Atlantic University, Florida Gulf Coast
University, Florida International University, Florida
State University, New College of Florida, University
of Central Florida, University of Florida, University
of North Florida, University of South Florida, and
University of West Florida.

University Press of Florida
15 Northwest 15th Street
Gainesville, FL 32611-2079
http://upress.ufl.edu

Para Tata, Mami, Kristina, y Sarah

Contents

Recipe List

DESSERTS

DRINKS

My Puerto Rican Kitchen

WHEN I WAS EIGHTEEN, I moved out of my mom's house into an apartment with roommates, and I promptly went to the closest grocery store and stocked my pantry with the ingredients Mami always had on hand: Goya Sazón packets, pimento-stuffed manzanilla olives, canned garbanzos, white rice, raisins, olive oil, dried oregano, coconut milk, tomato sauce, and tons of garlic and onions. It wasn't until I started cooking for my friends that I realized that these ingredients and the flavors they produced were uncommon.

Most of the ingredients you'll need to stock your Puerto Rican pantry can be found at your average grocery store, often in the international or "Mexican" section. Mexican, Latino, and general farmers' markets are good places to look for specialty items, in particular root vegetables, herbs, and spices.

The foundations of Puerto Rican cuisine lie in a handful of aromatic spice pastes and blends, handmade broths, and coconut milk. Below are the basics you'll need to stock your Puerto Rican pantry and the recipes for the signature ingredients that will give your dishes that unique Puerto Rican flavor.

INGREDIENTS

Achiote (**annatto**): *Achiote* is a seed that is ground and used widely in Puerto Rican food to add color and a mild earthiness to various dishes. Ground or whole *achiote* can be difficult to find in supermarkets but can be ordered from online spice stores. Otherwise mild sweet paprika makes a good substitute.

Aguacate (**avocado**): No Puerto Rican meal is complete without a plate of avocado slices, lightly salted and sometimes drizzled with olive oil. On the U.S. mainland we're more accustomed to small, dark green Hass avocados, which have concentrated flavor. But in Puerto Rico it's more common to find

the large, bright green, smooth-skinned avocados that are big enough to fill your hand. They have a milder, slightly sweeter flavor, and pair incredibly with Puerto Rican flavors.

Ají dulce **chiles:** *Dulce* means sweet, and even though *ají dulce* looks deceptively like a Scotch bonnet or habanero chile, it is a sweet chile. When purchasing, be very careful you're buying the right thing. When in doubt, or if you can't find *ají dulce*, simply use an equal amount of yellow, orange, or red bell pepper.

Calabaza **(pumpkin):** This pumpkin is not like the tough-skinned orange pumpkin you carve for Halloween. It's more similar in flavor to a kabocha squash. The skin has a sweet flavor and becomes soft enough to eat when cooked.

Capers: Growing up, my mother was strongly salt averse, and so she never used capers in her food. I, on the other hand, am salt obsessed and can't get enough of these briny, tart, salty pickles. As a rule, I prefer smaller capers packed in brine for Puerto Rican dishes.

Chayote: Often thought of as a squash, chayotes are actually in the gourd family and look like knobby, bright-green pears. They have a mild, delicate flavor and can be eaten raw, blanched, stuffed with meat and cheese, or stir-fried with eggs and spices. They're commonly found in Mexican grocery stores and are regionally available in your average grocery store.

Chicharrón: Crispy fried pork skins come in a number of different forms in Puerto Rico and are a far cry from the kind you get in

a bag at the gas station. *Chicharrón volao* is airy, super-crispy salted fried skin that has an incredible crunch. What's often called *chicharrón Dominicano* has a bit of the meat still attached and is a little fattier, chewier, and much meatier. Both are delicious, and you can decide which you'd prefer to use in a recipe. It's most often found in Latino markets, or if you live in a community with Puerto Ricans, Dominicans, or Cubans, you can also find it at a *cuchifrito* stand where they sell other fried goodies.

Chimichurri: This is a traditional Argentinian condiment, often found in clay pots on the table like we might have ketchup in the United States. It's incredibly versatile and flavorful, adding a strong punch of raw garlic, grassy oil, and bright herbs to grilled meat or roasted vegetables. See my recipe on page 34.

Cilantro: Fresh cilantro is more commonly cooked into dishes than used as a garnish, but I like to use it both ways.

Citrus juice: In all my recipes, lemon, lime, and orange juice should always be freshly squeezed.

Cotija cheese: This crumbled cow's milk cheese—somewhere between Parmesan and cottage cheese in flavor—is commonly used in Mexican food. Puerto Rican food doesn't use cheese very often (at least the way my family cooked), but I find that *cotija* works well as a garnish for soups and salads.

Culantro: Also called *recao,* culantro can be very difficult to find. It tastes as if parsley and cilantro had a baby, so if culantro is unavailable, you can substitute half cilantro and half parsley.

Gandules **(pigeon peas):** These legumes are coveted in Puerto Rican food, including in one of the most popular rice dishes—*arroz con gandules,* or rice with pigeon peas. The popularity of *gandules* is attributed to their nutty, earthy deliciousness. They have a distinct flavor that tastes nothing like a typical black, red, or white bean and are elevated by cooking in *sofrito* or with pork.

Garbanzos (chickpeas): Stewed garbanzos, cooked with stock, *sofrito,* and perhaps a bit of pork, are a typical simple, affordable Puerto Rican dish. Garbanzos are also incorporated into stews and meat braises.

Garlic: If there's a single flavor that savory Puerto Rican dishes share, it's garlic. When I first began experimenting with classic Puerto Rican recipes, I found that nearly all of them used an inordinate amount of garlic. Don't get me wrong, I love garlic. But I found that oftentimes the amount used in my favorite dishes was overkill, as if intended to cover up subpar ingredients. The recipes in this book use garlic moderately, so augment at will.

Guayaba **(guava):** This fragrant fruit is the epitome of tropical flavor. Guava has a unique floral, tangy sweetness and is—in my opinion—the most delicious fruit on the planet. Guava is either tennis ball–size, green on the outside, and bright salmon pink on the inside, or golf ball–size with pale yellow skin and white flesh. Both contain

dozens of round white seeds in the center, which shouldn't be eaten.

Leche de coco (coconut milk): Although it's a project to make, no canned milk or milk in a carton comes close to the bright, floral taste of homemade coconut milk. See page 15 for my recipe.

Ñame: A type of white sweet potato that's decidedly less sweet than the garnet yams we're more accustomed to on the U.S. mainland and firmer and earthier in flavor. Ñame can be difficult to find; you can substitute Japanese white sweet potato and reduce the cooking time.

Olive oil: For the recipes in this cookbook, use mild extra virgin olive oil, more on the fruity spectrum than strong and grassy.

Oregano: Oregano is the exclusive dried herb of traditional Puerto Rican cuisine. Fresh oregano works well in some dishes but can also be sharp and aggressive, whereas dried oregano provides an herbal balance to braised dishes.

Pimento-stuffed manzanilla olives: Among the strongest signals of Spanish influence on Puerto Rican food, tangy, briny pimento-stuffed olives find their way into many Puerto Rican dishes, in particular braised meats and stews. If they're not available, other types of green olives can be substituted.

Plátanos **(plantains—green and yellow):** Synonymous with Caribbean cuisines, plantains are among the cornerstones of Puerto Rican cooking. They show up in all kinds of ways. Green plantains are fried and mashed into disks called *tostones* that are eaten along with garlic or hot sauce or used in place of bread to sop up broths and sauces. Yellow, spotted sweet plantains, or *maduros*, are often fried and served alongside a variety of dishes to provide that sweet-savory fix. They are also mashed and formed into Puerto Rican shepherd's pie or can be oven-roasted with butter, brown sugar, and cinnamon. See pages 82 and 74 for my recipes.

Queso de hoja **and** *queso fresco***:** These cow's-milk cheeses are commonly found on the island, sometimes stuffed into pastries or empanadas but most often eaten alone as a snack alongside *pasta de guayaba* (guava paste).

Salt: Unless otherwise specified, use kosher salt for the recipes in this book.

Spanish chorizo: Distinct from Mexican chorizo, which is most often found fresh in the meat department of grocery stores, Spanish chorizo is firm, cured sausage that is intensely flavorful and variably spicy. If you can't find it at your local grocery store, you may find it at a specialty butcher.

Tomatoes: As I was researching traditional Puerto Rican recipes, I found that most called for tomato sauce instead of fresh tomatoes. My grandmother would often serve fresh tomatoes, but they were nearly always tasteless, refrigerated tomatoes doused in olive oil. In my recipes, I recommend using red, ripe, off-the-vine tomatoes or plum tomatoes. If not available, substitute whole, peeled canned tomatoes.

Vinegar: The flavor profile of many Puerto Rican dishes includes some kind of acid, either citrus juice or vinegar. White vinegar is traditionally used, but red and white wine vinegars also work.

Yautía: Also called *malanga* or taro root, yautía is one of the richest, most flavorful root vegetables in Puerto Rican cooking. It can be white, yellow, or *lila* (light purple), with a dry, hairy skin. When boiled, as when it's incorporated in stews like *sancocho* or mashed in *una majada*, it has a creamy, buttery texture but with a singular funkiness. It's by far my favorite root.

Yucca: These large, wax-skinned tubers are eaten across the Caribbean and Africa. They are most commonly deep-fried and served with a sauce such as mayo-ketchup, boiled and served with sautéed onions, garlic, and olive oil, or cooked in stews.

BASICS

Sofrito

What I'm calling *sofrito* is sometimes referred to as *recaito*, the distinction being whether or not it includes tomato. But the basic ingredients are the same. It is the number one backbone of Puerto Rican cooking and can be adapted in a number of ways depending on the dish. Abuelitas and tias alike often keep *sofrito* in the freezer stored in repurposed plastic margarine containers or frozen into cubes and saved in zip-top bags. It's best used within a week if kept in the refrigerator but can be frozen for up to six months. Plop it in the pan straight out of the freezer to save time defrosting it.

Makes 3 cups

1 medium red bell pepper, seeded and quartered

3 *ají dulce* chiles, seeded and roughly chopped

6 large garlic cloves, peeled

1 large yellow onion, coarsely chopped

6 fresh culantro leaves

6 fresh cilantro leaves and stems, coarsely chopped

Put the bell pepper, *ají dulce* chiles, and garlic cloves in the bowl of a food processor and blend into a smooth puree, scraping the sides halfway through to incorporate fully.

Add the onion and pulse 5 to 7 times, until the mixture is again blended into a smooth puree.

Add the culantro and cilantro and pulse 5 or 6 more times, until the stems and leaves are minced and you have a loose paste.

Adobo

To *adobar* or season/marinate meat is what gives much Puerto Rican food its signature flavor. As a rule, marinating should be done as far in advance as possible—preferably overnight—but it's still delicious if you only have thirty minutes to spare. This is a very adaptable marinade. If you love garlic, add more. If you prefer lime juice to lemon juice, use it. Recipes are for chicken, seafood, beef, or pork but are mostly interchangeable. A series of recommendations for other adjustments, such as adding smoked paprika to give depth and color, are included with individual recipes. Traditionally, an *adobo* is ground in a wooden *pilón* (or mortar and pestle), but like my mother, I use a food processor because it's quick and easy.

Adobo for Chicken and Seafood (for each pound of meat)

1 medium garlic clove, finely minced

⅛ teaspoon freshly ground black pepper

½ teaspoon dried oregano

1 teaspoon salt

1 teaspoon olive oil

½ teaspoon fresh lemon juice

Adobo for Pork (for each pound of meat)

1 medium garlic clove, finely minced

⅛ teaspoon ground black pepper

½ teaspoon dried oregano

1 teaspoon salt

1 teaspoon olive oil

½ teaspoon fresh lime, lemon, or sour orange juice

Adobo for Beef (for each pound of meat)

1 medium garlic clove, finely minced

¼ teaspoon ground black pepper

½ teaspoon dried oregano

1 teaspoon salt

1 teaspoon olive oil

1 teaspoon fresh lime juice, or white or red wine vinegar

Note: Each recipe is per pound of meat, and all salt is measured in teaspoons. Meat should always be rinsed with cold water and thoroughly dried with paper towels before rubbing down with *adobo*. The best way to store *carne adobada* (seasoned meat) overnight is in a large, heavy-duty zip-top bag or tightly wrapped in plastic wrap.

Put all the ingredients in the bowl of a small food processor and blend into a smooth puree, scraping the sides halfway through to incorporate fully.

Sazón

Maybe you've seen those orange boxes of Goya Sazón at your local grocery store. It's a miracle ingredient, a punch of MSG with enough other spices to flavor just about any soup, stew, bean dish, or braise. It's an incredible cheat, and so full of sodium it might give you a migraine. I'll admit that I have a box in my pantry right now in case of emergency. But I think you can do better.

Makes 8 tablespoons (½ cup)

1 tablespoon garlic powder

1 tablespoon onion powder

1 tablespoon ground cumin

1 tablespoon ground turmeric

½ teaspoon ground black pepper

2 tablespoons salt

2 tablespoons ground *achiote* or sweet paprika

Combine all the ingredients in an airtight container, cover, and shake well to incorporate. It keeps indefinitely.

Caldos (Stocks)

The base stock for Puerto Rican soups, stews, and beans is an unusual combination of ingredients that are bright, earthy, and robust. As with any other stock, it's a great way to use up reserved vegetable trimmings, bones, and seafood shells.

Makes about 2 quarts

Beef and Pork Stock

2 pounds beef or pork trimmings

2 pounds beef or pork bones

5 quarts water

2 tablespoons salt

2 onions, peeled and quartered

2 tomatoes, halved

1 green bell pepper, seeded and quartered

1 red bell pepper, seeded and quartered

4 *ají dulce* chiles

6 fresh culantro leaves

6 fresh cilantro stems

2 ears of corn, husked

4 garlic cloves

Vegetable Stock

5 quarts water

2 tablespoons salt

2 onions, peeled and quartered

2 carrots, halved

2 celery stalks, halved

2 tomatoes, halved

1 green bell pepper, seeded and quartered

1 red bell pepper, seeded and quartered

4 *ají dulce* chiles

6 fresh culantro leaves

6 fresh cilantro stems

2 ears of corn, husked

4 garlic cloves

Shrimp Stock

4 cups (about 1 pound) whole shrimp or shrimp shells

5 quarts water

2 tablespoons salt

2 onions, peeled and quartered

2 carrots, halved

2 celery stalks, halved

2 tomatoes, halved

6 *ají dulce* chiles

6 fresh culantro leaves

3 ears of corn, husked

6 garlic cloves

½ teaspoon whole black peppercorns

4 bay leaves

Combine all the ingredients in a large stockpot, cover, and bring to a boil over high heat.

Reduce heat to low and cook at a low simmer for 2 hours.

Remove from the heat, cool slightly, then strain through a fine-mesh sieve. Set aside until ready to use, or let cool fully, then transfer to a tight-lidded container for storage. It keeps for up to 1 week in the refrigerator and several months in the freezer.

Leche de Coco (Coconut Milk)

It's a laborious process, an experiment for over the weekend, maybe with a few friends in the mix. But trust me, fresh coconut milk is worth it. It will keep in the refrigerator for up to 1 week and freezes well.

Makes 4 cups

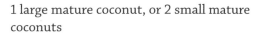

1 large mature coconut, or 2 small mature coconuts

3 cups hot water

Carefully crack or drill a hole in the coconut using a hammer and a screwdriver or a power drill and pour the coconut water through a fine-mesh sieve into a container. Most coconuts yield about ¾ cup water.

Split the coconut in half. Remove the tough outer shell, then peel the dark skin off the coconut meat. Rinse thoroughly, dry, then grate using the grating attachment of a food processor if available, or a box grater.

Combine the grated coconut with the hot water and reserved coconut water. Mix well and press with a potato masher or through a ricer to get out all of the coconut milk. Set the coconut meat aside.

Pour the coconut milk through a fine-mesh sieve. You should have 4 cups of coconut milk. (If you're short, add a bit more warm water to the grated coconut and press again.)

Introduction

It's Puerto Rican Because I Made It

Mi abuela tenía una teoría muy interesante; decía que todos nacemos con una caja de fósforos adentro, pero que no podemos encenderlos solos . . . necesitamos la ayuda del oxígeno y una vela. . . . Ese fuego . . . es su alimento. Si uno no averigua a tiempo qué cosa inicia esas explosiones, la caja de fósforos se humedece y ni uno solo de los fósforos se encenderá nunca.

My grandmother had a very interesting theory. She said that each of us is born with a box of matches inside us, but we can't light them by ourselves; we need oxygen and a candle to help. . . . That fire . . . is its food. If you don't figure out what will set these tiny explosions off in time, the box of matches dampens, and not a single match will ever be lighted.

—Laura Esquivel, *Como Agua Para Chocolate (Like Water for Chocolate)*

What constitutes "good food," like what constitutes good weather, a good spouse, or a fulfilling life, is a social, not a biological matter. Good food . . . must be good to think about before it becomes good to eat.

—Sidney Mintz, *Sweetness and Power*

I'm a terrible salsa dancer.

Rice . . . doesn't excite me.

I'm prone to saying "y'all" and "ma'am."

And, I'm Puerto Rican.

When I was a little girl, my family moved from Río Piedras, Puerto Rico, to Atlanta, Georgia, and I traded plantains, roast pork, and malta for grits, fried chicken, and sweet tea. But Puerto Rican food is my lifeline to the island and the way I stay connected to a culture that is fundamental to who I am.

The food my family eats and the way we cook reflect multiple migrations back and forth from the Caribbean to the American South. It also reflects the way a cook—in this case my grandmother, Tata—can serve as an ambassador of taste. Tata's cooking did more than nourish; her food was a party, a celebration, a love letter. At its best, she cooked as a way to bring people together, to create community. And, I believe, to express something deeper that she felt.

The intoxicating, seductive food she made and the *way* she cooked inspired me to start cooking through her 1962 copy of *Cocina Criolla*—a cookbook that many consider to

be the Puerto Rican *Joy of Cooking*. Its recipes are a fusion of 1950s American ingredients (think mayonnaise and canned veggies) with African deep-frying techniques, indigenous Taíno root vegetables, and a Spanish obsession with olive oil, garlic, and pork.

Today I can say the journey that sprang from the oil-stained pages of that cookbook has been surprising and deeply rewarding. But it didn't start out that way. Like so many low-income households headed by single mothers, mine required that I learn to cook at a young age and to improvise using limited ingredients. I am a self-taught home cook trained largely by my mother and grandmother (and the Internet). I rely largely on my senses and instincts to tell me when something looks and tastes right. Oftentimes it ends with delicious meals. But I've had my share of mishaps along the way.

Like the time I made a *pavochón*, a Puerto Rican–style turkey seasoned like a pork roast and stuffed with *mofongo*, or green plantains fried then smashed with garlic and *chicharrón*, or fried pork skins. I could barely fit the turkey in my tiny fridge to marinate it overnight, much less fit it in my oven, so I took a cab forty blocks to my friends' apartment in Washington Heights to roast it. It was delicious, crazy delicious, but it basically took me three full days to plan and prepare.

Next, I tried to make homemade coconut milk in my nine-foot-by-nine-foot Manhattan kitchen using a power drill and a hammer—knocking bits of coconut bark so far I found them under and in things for months. Not to mention stripping my drill bit and chipping the end of my best knife. The end result was sumptuous, floral, and delicate

(you'll find a revised, apartment-ready machete-less coconut milk recipe on page 15), but it was hard to justify the labor.

These humbling endeavors taught me a lot. I am not, and have no desire to be, a 1960s Puerto Rican housewife. I do not own a machete, nor do I have a big patio where I can whack dried coconuts. But I do want to create simple food that's satisfying, healthy, *and* full of flavor.

Reflecting on my background made me think hard about what I eat, why I eat it, and what it takes to make every meal you put in your mouth delicious. Sometimes that means lightening it up, adding fresh herbs and vegetables. Sometimes that means frying it in lard. You have to try it out and

decide for yourself. With history and culture as your guides, the path to creating delicious foods that make you and those around you smile can be incredibly joyful and can reveal connections to your past and to others that you wouldn't otherwise see.

And so *Cocina Criolla* is the inspiration and foundation for this book—but ultimately a culinary legacy I aim to evolve. Because, like many granny cookbooks with their pages splattered with sauce and scribbled with notes, it reflects an old way of eating.

Puerto Rico became a Spanish colony more than five hundred years ago. The majority of indigenous Taínos were rapidly killed or enslaved, and huge communities of enslaved Africans were brought to the island to work the fields and sugar plantations, as were indigenous communities from South America and Central America. The surviving Taínos taught these enslaved people how they cooked and what grew on the island, and Africans shared ingredients and techniques from their home countries, like plantains and rice and making flavorful pastes by grinding spices and deep-frying meat for preservation.

Food reflects so much about where we come from, and even more about who we want to be. Today, Puerto Rican food mirrors the history and struggles of its people. The island has been a U.S. territory for more than one hundred years, and economic and racial inequalities persist. And much like farming and working-class communities across the world, Puerto Rican cuisine reflects both a lack of access to vegetables and healthy ingredients and a subsequent reliance on making things heavy and filling.

But these same combinations, born of necessity and fusion, also create a uniquely Caribbean flavor profile that is rife with potential. Tender beef with sweet plump raisins and briny pimento-stuffed olives; funky, earthy root vegetables in pork stock, brightened by sweet peppers, corn, and cilantro; tropical guava, mango, and passion fruit blended with rich cream and burnt brown sugar; vegetal green plantains with crispy pork skins. These are the flavors I'm obsessed with, that inspire me to keep exploring and adapting my island's cuisine.

Food is social. Food is personal. Eating is a common act that is also deeply complex and full of possibilities. Those possibilities are what excite me. So I didn't give up after that puddle of coconut milk on the kitchen floor or the fifty-dollar cab ride to roast a turkey. Instead I started thinking about what else *sofrito* would be good in (the answer is: basically everything). I began to make what now seem like obvious connections between the food I'd primarily grown up around—Southern food—and the African and indigenous influence in so many of Puerto Rico's dishes (*funche,* or grits, okra, fried chicken, fatback in your veggies).

And sometimes I'd make something completely my own and use culantro instead of cilantro and *ají dulce* chiles instead of bell peppers and decide I'd made something Puerto Rican. It was Puerto Rican because I made it. This book is a collection of the best of those explorations.

Just as I dug deep into the history of the island and its flavor profile, I also dug deep into my own personal history. Today, when I'm not cooking, eating, or thinking about

food, I'm also a radio producer and journalist. And so this book is just as much about stories as it is about cooking. Each chapter reflects how the women in my family—myself included—have used food to nourish and care for one another and to adapt to their surroundings and bodily needs. *Las mujeres de mi familia* (the women in my family) have been fierce survivors, and the steadiest metric for the good and the bad in our lives has always been measured by how well we're eating. There are magical elements in many of these stories that I cannot (and do not care to) verify because they are my truth, the way I understand my past.

The first chapter, "La Cocina de Tata," highlights traditional dishes, updated and lightened whenever possible (or necessary). Recipes include *pescado en escabeche* (chilled pickled white fish), *sancocho* (a kitchen-sink stew brimming with meats and root vegetables), and my Mami's rum cake. In it you'll learn my grandmother's story: escaping the Dominican Republic as a child, landing in Biloxi, Mississippi, and ending up in Altamesa, Puerto Rico, where *my* story begins.

Chapter 2, "Mofongo Blues," takes you to some not-so-beautiful suburbs outside of Atlanta, Georgia, where I grew up and learned to see the deep connections between the place where I was born and the one I'd come to call home. It also pays homage to a sweet Southern mama named Miss Donna, who taught me how good Southern food *could* be, while also looking at the strong connection between eating and loss.

"Nosotras," the third chapter, tells the story of how I came to cook as a way to care for my family, emotionally and physically.

You'll get to know my mother, whom I call Mami (though her name is Yvonne), at one of the most difficult times in her life. But you'll also see her for the lioness she is, protecting her pride and keeping us from falling apart at a moment when we might have splintered.

And the final chapter, "Retorno," brings you to the present day, where my connection to the island grew strong as a result of an extremely painful moment in my life. It's about me, but it's about all of my women, and how they formed a protective aura around me that continues to give me life. And about how food prepared for you by caring hands can be a healing balm like no other.

What you won't find in this book: *mofongo, léchon,* or *cuchifritos* (well, only one). Don't get me wrong, I love these foods, but I don't eat them regularly.

What you will find in this book: coconut *funche* (grits), plantain-crusted shrimp, and Brussels sprouts with chorizo *sofrito*. Because my goal has always been to make food I actually want to cook and eat.

The recipes in this book were tested entirely by my community; some home cooks like me, some trained chefs, some folks who were excited to learn about an unknown cuisine. And so I encourage adaptation and sharing. Ultimately I trust that every cook knows best what tastes good to them, the limitations and opportunities in their kitchens and tools, and what they're comfortable cooking.

This book is my take on one family's history and an entire island's cuisine in a handful of recipes. I hope you enjoy them. Buen provecho.

1

La Cocina de Tata

I had my last guava the day we left Puerto Rico. It was large and juicy, almost red in the center, and so fragrant that I didn't want to eat it because I would lose the smell. All the way to the airport I scratched at it with my teeth, making little dents in the skin, chewing small pieces with my front teeth so I could feel the texture against my tongue, the tiny pink pellets of sweet.

—Esmeralda Santiago, *When I Was Puerto Rican*

ALREADY AN INSOMNIAC AT AGE ELEVEN, I had a hard enough time sleeping in my air-conditioned room back home in Georgia. Now in Puerto Rico, I was on a hard mattress on the floor, with a rusty box fan blowing hot air across my body. It was impossible to sleep there. Most nights I just stared at the cracks in the ceiling and worried. *How many awkward conversations in broken Spanish will I have? Who's going to make fun of how gringa I am?*

It was my second full summer in PR, and things at home were a mess. The last thing I remembered before getting on the plane— this is back when folks could take you all the way to the gate—was the dark circles under my mother's eyes and my little sister sobbing.

I hadn't wanted to go to Puerto Rico that summer. I wanted to stay home, watch television, and hang out in the playground with the other kids in our apartment complex. But my mom couldn't afford camp and I was too old for day care, so I was shipped off to PR . . . to suffer. My parents had split up earlier that year, and—still in the Army at that time—Papi had been given orders to go to Korea. He'd already been pretty absent, but he was literally on the other side of the world from me at that time.

It wasn't *all* bad. I liked traveling, and the beach, and (most of) my family. But more than anything else on the island, I *loved* Puerto Rican food and my grandmother Tata. And as I reluctantly boarded the plane, my thoughts turned to *bacalaítos, alcapurrias, aguacates,* and *chicharrón.* And Tata, my favorite person in the world, was a beacon of light in my otherwise dismal prepubescence.

On that particular morning in Altamesa, sweaty and miserable, I let a smile creep across my face because it was

✦ 27

Saturday—Tata's day off. I caught a whiff of her Benson & Hedges cigarettes and the pungent, burnt smell of the *cafetera* sputtering. I got up, put on my pink plastic-rimmed glasses and my *chancletas*, and shuffled out to greet her.

Tata was standing in the living room wearing a loose-fitting pink cotton tank top and pale orange shorts, her hair in rollers, a cigarette in her mouth as she finished her morning routine. She'd already watered the dozen or so plants on her *marquesina* (front patio) and hosed down and squeegeed the tile floors and concrete walls.

Her *marquesina* was a mini botanical garden. Seven spider plants hung side by side on the railing, their leaves making it difficult to see the street. The floor, side tables, and shelves were covered with potted ferns, bromeliads, and philodendrons. The entire porch was surrounded with a decorative grate painted white, its bars forming an intricate interlocking geometric pattern. Its front door was wound with a heavy-duty steel chain and two padlocks because she'd been robbed four times in the last three years. The wooden cocktail bar against the right side of the porch, facing the street, was decorated with figurines, photographs, and paintings of Boxers, her favorite dog, which she spent much of my mother's early childhood breeding, training, and exhibiting.

"*Ay, mira quien está despierta!*" (Look who's awake!), Tata said, giving me a toothy smile. I learned later those weren't her real teeth. "*Que te preparo?*" (What can I make for you?)

Because I never slept well, I rarely woke up hungry. But when I was in Puerto Rico, I ate whenever there was food.

"*No se Tata,*" I replied slyly, with a yawn. "*Que hay?*"

"*Conflake?*"

"No . . ." I replied.

"*Una tostada con jelly?*"

"Eh, no. I'm not really hungry. Don't worry about me," I lied.

"*Ay, yo sé!*" she said, her eyebrows bouncing mischievously. "*Un sanguich de picadillo!*"

A meat sandwich for breakfast?! Yes.

Most folks are familiar with a handful of Puerto Rican foods. *Mofongo*, *pernil*, and *picadillo*. If you don't know the last, it's ground beef cooked with *sofrito* and other spices, with green olives and (sometimes) raisins added. It's often stuffed into empanadas and other *cuchifritos* (deep-fried snacks), but my grandmother always kept some on hand like other folks keep lunchmeat. And I usually just ate it straight out of the fridge—cold, with a spoon.

I sat on a bar stool at the counter and watched her carefully orchestrated movements. Tata's kitchen was incredibly modest—only slightly larger than the one I would later have in my early thirties in New York's East Harlem, with one counter, a small sink, and a four-burner gas range. She spread butter on a piece of white sandwich bread, then placed it in the center of a sandwich press. Next came a slice of Kraft American cheese, a heaping scoop of *picadillo*, and another slice of cheese. Then she topped it all off with more buttered bread and pulled down the press handle to toast. The whole time I talked, telling her about my latest dream, mouth watering as I rattled on to pass the time. She opened the press and there were two perfect triangles with crisped edges, the caramelized filling clinging to tiny eruptions in the bread.

I marveled at how a woman born in the Dominican Republic, who lived most of her life in Puerto Rico, could make what was ultimately a perfect grilled cheese sandwich. But then I remembered her roots.

Tata was born Sara Canario Linares in the Dominican Republic in 1936, when Rafael Trujillo was at the height of his power. My great-grandfather Faustino was the owner of Santo Domingo Motors, which was one of the only car dealerships in the DR at the time. One night, when my grandmother was six years old, three men came to the house and shot her father. She, along with her mother and sister, Zora (whose mother was their housekeeper, though they had the same father), fled the country in the trunk of a Cadillac and ended up in Biloxi, Mississippi, where two of her aunts lived. She spent most of her childhood and teenage years living in that small coastal town in the Deep South.

Her life after was a whirlwind. She studied pre-med at Loyola in New Orleans, had a short-lived marriage to an Italian military officer that resulted in my aunt Sara, and ultimately landed her in Puerto Rico—where she lived most of her life. And where she became the best cook in the world.

That morning in Puerto Rico, we returned to the *marquesina,* me with my breakfast on a small white plate and Tata with a cigarette and a strong, sugary, black cup of coffee. I took a bite of my *sanguich* and molten cheese burst out of its toasty, buttery casing, burning the roof of my mouth with creamy, salty-sweet filling. I didn't care.

The air was hot and thick with the smells of car exhaust and hot asphalt, coffee, cigarette smoke, and cheesy meat. I took another bite and got a briny pimento-stuffed olive, a sweet, plump black raisin in the next. Tata watched me intently, with the eyes of a chef who knows a good eater. I chattered on in broken Spanglish between bites, because I'd been practicing my Spanish and she spoke perfect English.

I finished, wiping off my beaming, euphoric face with a paper towel. She smiled slyly.

"Quieres otra?"(Do you want another?), she asked.

I was stuffed and wasn't even hungry to begin with. "Si," I replied, grinning.

The rest of my summer in Puerto Rico went pretty much the same. Folks fed me too much; I ate everything and got round.

But when I wasn't eating or talking to Tata (or both), I was pretty miserable. I sulked, complained, sat as close to the fan as I could, craved TV, read *Jurassic Park* for the fifth time, and become agoraphobic. Kids my age and adults alike constantly mocked my shitty Spanish, and even though they jokingly said my mispronunciations and misused words were cute, they also laughed at me when I used *usted* instead of *tu*. When I went to stores by myself, I never seemed to move fast enough, and cashiers would impatiently yell at me so rapidly that I couldn't figure out what I had done.

The island seemed to be against me. I was constantly sunburned, whereas my family members never even seemed to get pink. Mosquitoes loved me, even biting my eyelids. The oppressive heat made me sweat constantly, which meant I was always self-conscious, grumpy, and exhausted. It all made me feel incredibly insecure and alone on the island where I was born but no longer felt I belonged—although I wanted to badly.

But Tata seemed to get it, and she understood that food was a way home for me and a strong bond between us. In many ways, I think food was a similar comfort for her.

That summer, she started teaching me how to cook well. I had some basics under my belt, but she took me on a journey full of new discoveries. First, she let me make *mojo caliente,* a warm sauce made by mashing garlic and salt in a *pilón,* or wooden mortar and pestle. Together we brought olive oil to a low simmer and she showed me how to carefully pour the oil into the *pilón*; garlic sizzled, filling the air with its smell and that of seasoned wood. We added lime juice and black pepper and saved it for dinner when we'd pour it over yucca or dip in some bread.

Each day, she showed me something new. She drove out of the way to get the best *mantecaditos*—a cookie similar to shortbread, often made with lard and decorated with rainbow sprinkles—from a hidden bakery in Guaynabo, and took me all the way to the coast to have *alcapurrias de langosta*, a root vegetable fritter stuffed with lobster.

On one of those weekend trips to Luquillo, Tata spotted a *kiosko,* or roadside food stand, along the highway and said it looked like a good one.

"Why this one?" I asked. It was barely a shack; four wooden poles held up a thatched palm leaf roof and a limp sign read COCO FRESCO, BACALAÍTOS. A man and woman sat in white plastic chairs under the shade of a palm tree next to a large bin filled with ice and green coconuts, their little shack outfitted with two deep fryers.

"Tu ves ahí" (You see there), she said. "They only have coco and *bacalaítos*. That means they're experts at that."

We pulled over, palm trees lining the road to our left, the coastline peeking through. I leapt out of the car and was hit with a burst of salty sea air. The vendors looked in my direction, startled by this enthusiastic child running full-speed toward their stand.

"*Un bacalaíto, por favor,*" I said, breathless, having perfected that phrase.

"*Uno nada más?*" the vendor asked, winking. How did he *know*?

Bacalaítos are flat, salty codfish funnel cakes—crisped and golden brown on the outside, moist and chewy on the inside. The batter is subtly sweet with a hint of funky fishiness that accentuates the sweet/savory that is such a signature of Puerto Rican food.

We walked across the highway to the ocean, taking our fritters and coconuts with us. The vendor had cut the tops off our coconuts and sliced pieces of hard shell off the sides for us to use as scoops. We sipped from our coconuts, then scooped bits of coconut meat out, licking our fingers. The fresh coconut meat tasted more like avocado than sweetened grated coconut—creamy, rich, and barely sweet.

Tata and I sat side by side on the sand and looked out past the sea. If I have one regret, it's that I didn't share more with her about what was going on in my life back home and how much I struggled to feel like I belonged on the island. I wanted so badly for her to think I was okay. And maybe part of me thought that if I stuffed myself with Puerto Rican food, with *her* food, I could somehow unlock the secrets of that place, that identity, its history, and this nagging sense that I belonged there even though it didn't seem to want me. I think she would have understood what I was going through much better than I could have imagined.

RECIPES

The recipes in this chapter are largely adaptations of classic Puerto Rican dishes. They are inspired by cookbooks including *Cocina Criolla* (Carmen Aboy Valldejuli, 1954), *Cocine a Gusto* (Berta Cabanillas, 1954), and *Cocinando en San Germán* (Marina Martínez de Irizarry, 1989), as well as my family's home recipes. My goal for this chapter (and the rest of the book as well) is to lighten up heavy dishes and make the flavors brighter and more balanced.

If you're looking for the kinds of meals a Puerto Rican abuela might have made, here's where you'll find them. You can pick and choose from among these recipes or make a fabulous, complete classic Puerto Rican banquet.

Culantro Chimichurri

Salsa Ajili-Mojili

Picadillo

Sanguiches de Picadillo (Picadillo Sandwiches)

Brussels Sprouts with Chorizo Sofrito

Sancocho

Boliche (Chorizo-Stuffed Beef Roast)

Chuletas a la Jardinera
(Pork Chops with Garden Vegetables)

Pescado en Escabeche (White Fish Escabeche)

Buñuelos de Viento en Almibar (Fried Doughnuts in
Cinnamon Syrup)

Pie de Limón (Lemon Meringue Pie)

Mami's Bizcocho de Ron (Mami's Rum Cake)

Coquito (Coconut Eggnog)

Culantro Chimichurri

Tata loved vegetables *and* meat. One of her favorite condiments to have ready in the fridge or make on the fly was *chimichurri*. She often served it with green beans or Brussels sprouts and alongside a steak cooked medium-rare or a roast chicken. It's a great quick sauce you can use like Tata did, or with grilled vegetables and meat.

Makes 3½ cups

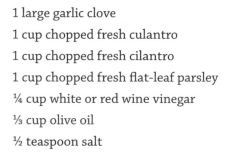

1 large garlic clove

1 cup chopped fresh culantro

1 cup chopped fresh cilantro

1 cup chopped fresh flat-leaf parsley

¼ cup white or red wine vinegar

⅓ cup olive oil

½ teaspoon salt

Place the garlic in a small food processor and process to finely mince it.

Add the culantro, cilantro, parsley, vinegar, oil, and salt and pulse into a fine paste, scraping the sides as needed to make sure the ingredients are fully incorporated.

Scrape into a bowl and serve immediately.

Note: Chimichurri is best eaten the same day, though it will keep up to a week in the refrigerator (the color will change from bright green to brown after a few days).

Salsa Ajili-Mojili

This sauce is extremely versatile and pairs particularly well with steamed or lightly sautéed vegetables, avocado, white beans, and seafood. I've added a variation in honor of a good friend who has a garlic allergy, which is just as delicious and a good substitute if you don't enjoy raw garlic or want a milder flavor.

Makes 1½ cups

3 garlic cloves, minced (or 4 scallions, whites and greens, thinly sliced)

½ cup *ají dulce* chiles, seeded and finely chopped

2 tablespoons fresh lime juice

½ cup olive oil

1 teaspoon salt

⅛ teaspoon ground black pepper

Combine all the ingredients in a medium bowl and mix well. Let sit for at least 15 minutes or up to 1 hour before serving. It will keep in the refrigerator for up to a week, though it is best within the first couple days.

Picadillo

This was one of a handful of dishes always found in Tata's refrigerator. As a kid I would sneak into the kitchen at night when I couldn't sleep and eat it out of a container with a spoon. It can be eaten as a main course alongside rice and beans or root vegetables, but it's also commonly used as a stuffing in empanadas, fritters, and *pastelón*. I prefer turkey, but beef is traditional.

Makes 3 cups

2 tablespoons olive oil

½ cup Sofrito (page 10)

½ cup tomato sauce

1 tablespoon Sazón (page 12)

2 bay leaves

1 pound ground turkey or beef

¼ cup pimento-stuffed manzanilla olives, halved

1 tablespoon drained capers in brine

1 tablespoon raisins (optional)

½ teaspoon salt, or to taste

⅛ teaspoon ground black pepper, or to taste

Heat the oil in a large, deep sauté pan over medium-high heat. Add the sofrito and cook for 5 minutes, stirring frequently.

Add the tomato sauce, sazón, and bay leaves to the pan and cook for about 5 more minutes, stirring frequently, until the sauce darkens and the liquid is mostly evaporated.

Reduce the heat to medium and fold in the ground turkey, breaking it up and mixing it into the sauce. Cook, uncovered, stirring occasionally, for 10 minutes (15 minutes if using beef), or until the meat is fully browned, the liquid is completely reduced, and a thick sauce is created.

Add the olives, capers, raisins, salt, and pepper and cook for 2 more minutes to heat through. Taste and add more salt and pepper if needed.

Sanguiches de Picadillo (Picadillo Sandwiches)

This bomb of a breakfast sandwich will stay with you all day. It's decadent and incredibly flavorful. If you don't own a sandwich press, make it like you would a grilled cheese.

Makes 2 sandwiches

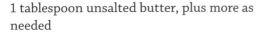

1 tablespoon unsalted butter, plus more as needed

4 slices white bread

4 slices American cheese

6 to 8 tablespoons Picadillo (page 36)

Butter one side of each slice of bread. Place 2 slices of bread, butter-side down, on a large plate.

Layer each of these 2 slices with one slice of American cheese, then top each with 3 to 4 tablespoons picadillo. Stack each with a second slice of American cheese. Top with the remaining bread slices, butter-side up.

Place in a sandwich press and cook until the cheese is melted, 3 to 5 minutes. The cheese may begin to creep out of the edges, which is okay.

Let rest for 1 minute before eating (the cheese is molten and can burn the roof of your mouth).

Brussels Sprouts with Chorizo Sofrito

Of all the things my grandmother cooked, the one that Mami said she hated and refused to eat was Brussels sprouts. It appears Tata used frozen, whole Brussels sprouts (likely the only ones she could find in Puerto Rico at the time). She would boil them and then toss in *chimichurri, salsa ajili-mojili,* or another sauce. Sadly, Tata was the only one who liked them. This recipe pays homage to Tata's good intentions. I think she would have loved it.

Serves 4 as a side

1½ tablespoons olive oil

¾ cup Sofrito (page 10)

½ cup finely minced Spanish chorizo

1 pound Brussels sprouts, trimmed and thinly sliced

½ cup chicken stock

1 teaspoon fresh lime juice

½ teaspoon salt, plus more if needed

Cracked black pepper

Heat the oil in a large skillet or wok over medium-high heat. Add the sofrito and chorizo and cook, stirring frequently, for 7 minutes, or until the mixture is browned and the liquid is mostly evaporated.

Lower the heat to medium and add the Brussels sprouts and stock. Bring to a simmer and cook for 7 to 10 minutes, until the Brussels sprouts are tender.

Turn off the heat, add the lime juice and salt, and season with pepper. Taste and adjust the salt and pepper if needed.

Sancocho

This stew is eaten across the Caribbean and has every imaginable variation. When I traveled to Cuba as a graduate student, I ate it at a *rumba* (an
all-day dance event based on Yoruba spiritual practices). There, it's called
ajiaco and is often served from a giant pot on the porch with a ladle,
meant to keep us all energized (or sober us up). In Puerto Rico, my family makes *sancocho* a number of different ways. My father makes his with
beef and noodles; Mami prefers chicken breasts and lean pork; Tata used
beef, chicken, and pork on the bone. Here's my take, but I encourage you
to adapt it to include whatever meats and vegetables you love.

Serves 8

1 medium yucca

1 medium yautía

1 green plantain

1 ripe yellow plantain

1 tablespoon olive oil

1 pound boneless chicken thighs

1 pound boneless pork stew meat, trimmed
of excess fat

½ cup Sofrito (page 10)

10 cups Beef and Pork Stock (page 13)

3 bay leaves

1 tablespoon salt

1 cup thinly sliced Spanish chorizo

2 cups 1-inch cubes peeled *calabaza*
(pumpkin) or kabocha squash

1 ear sweet corn, husk removed and cut into
1-inch slices

Peel and cut the yucca, yautía, green
plantain, and yellow plantain into 1-inch
pieces. Put in separate bowls, add water to
cover, and set aside until ready to use. This
keeps them from turning brown while you
prepare the rest of the soup.

In a large stockpot, heat the oil over
medium-high heat. Add the chicken and
cook until browned on both sides, about 5
minutes total. Remove to a plate. Add the
pork to the pan and cook until browned
on both sides, another 5 minutes or so.
Remove to the plate with the chicken.

Reduce the heat to medium and add the
sofrito to the same pot, scraping up any
browned bits of meat and incorporating them into the mix. Cook for 5 to 7
minutes, stirring frequently, until the
mixture is browned and the liquid is mostly
evaporated.

⟫⟶

Return the chicken and pork and any accumulated juices to the pot. Add the bay leaves and salt, increase the heat to medium-high, and bring to a boil. Reduce the heat to medium-low and simmer, uncovered, for about 10 minutes, stirring occasionally, until the stock is slightly reduced. Stir in the chorizo.

Add the remaining ingredients in order of firmness (to keep softer vegetables from falling apart), leaving each for 5 minutes before adding the next: First the yucca, then the yautía, followed by the green plantain, then the yellow plantain, pumpkin, and, finally, the corn, for a total of 30 minutes of cooking, or until the meat and vegetables are tender enough to break apart with a fork.

Remove from the heat, taste, and add more salt if needed. Serve with fresh bread or white rice on the side.

> *Note*: Root vegetables such as yucca and yautía can be difficult to find in basic supermarkets, though you may be able to find them in the freezer section. There's no real substitute for the rich, earthy flavor of these tubers, but potatoes can be used. Reduce the cooking time by half if using potatoes.

Boliche
(Chorizo-Stuffed Beef Roast)

My mother might as well be a vegetarian. Growing up she hated meat and was vocal about it. But on special occasions, Tata made *boliche*. It's a Cuban dish in which a whole eye-of-round roast is stuffed with a mixture of Spanish chorizo, *sofrito*, spices, and vegetables, then marinated overnight and braised. The end result is an incredibly tender, flavorful roast with a bright filling in the center that's gorgeous when served. To this day, if I even say the word *boliche*, my mother licks her lips.

Serves 8

6 garlic cloves, minced

1 teaspoon dried oregano

1 teaspoon ground cumin

1 bay leaf

1½ tablespoons fresh orange juice

1½ tablespoons fresh lime juice

1 cup dry white wine

2 teaspoons salt, or to taste

¼ teaspoon ground black pepper

1 red bell pepper, seeded and finely chopped

1 carrot, thinly sliced

2 small Spanish chorizos, thinly sliced

2 tablespoons vegetable oil

1 (5- to 6-pound) eye-of-round beef roast

1 (8-ounce) can tomato sauce

Prepare a marinade by combining the garlic, oregano, cumin, bay leaf, orange juice, lime juice, wine, salt, and pepper in a container large enough to hold the roast.

Place the bell pepper, carrot, and chorizos in a small bowl and toss to combine.

Trim the meat of excess fat, rinse it, and dry with a paper towel. Using a long knife with a sharp tip, slice into the roast lengthwise until you reach the other end. Cut through several more times from end to end, making an X-shaped cut and rotating the knife back and forth inside the cut to make space.

Place the roast in a large bowl, cut-side down, and stuff it with the chorizo mixture. Begin with about 1 tablespoon of the mixture and push in with your thumb, then use the end of a wooden spoon to push down farther. Rotate the roast to make sure both sides are equally stuffed. Place the roast in the container with the marinade,

turning several times to coat fully with the marinade, then return it to the refrigerator. Marinate for at least 1 hour, or overnight if possible.

Preheat the oven to 350°F. In a Dutch oven or heavy-bottomed saucepan with a cover, heat the oil over medium-high heat. Sear the meat for about 8 minutes total, until thoroughly browned on all four sides.

Add the marinade left from the meat, cover, and place in the oven for 2½ to 3 hours, until the meat is tender and falls apart easily when pierced with a fork. Transfer the meat to a cutting board and let rest for 5 minutes.

Meanwhile, add the tomato sauce to the marinade in the pot. Place over medium heat, bring to a simmer, and simmer for 3 to 4 minutes. Add any juices released from the meat while it is resting.

Carve the meat into ½-inch slices, divide among plates, and serve topped with the tomato sauce.

Pescado en Escabeche (White Fish Escabeche)

This is a great summer dish and perfect to make ahead of time for a brunch. Serve with a side salad, salted sliced tomatoes, avocado, or *tostones*.

Serves 4

Marinade

1 cup olive oil

½ cup white vinegar

¼ teaspoon ground black pepper

½ teaspoon salt

1 bay leaf

2 large white onions, sliced into thin rounds

Fish

1½ pounds grouper steaks

¼ cup fresh lemon juice (about 1 large lemon)

2 teaspoons salt, or to taste

¼ cup all-purpose flour

1 cup olive oil

Combine the marinade ingredients in a large bowl.

Line a large plate with paper towels and set it aside.

Rinse the fish well and pat dry with paper towels. Place the fish in a large bowl and pour the lemon juice over it. Sprinkle with the salt and toss well.

Pour the flour onto a large plate. One by one, dredge each fish steak in flour and transfer them to a separate plate.

Heat the oil in a large skillet over medium-high heat until just simmering, about 1 minute. Do not overheat the oil, or it will burn and turn bitter. Reduce the heat to medium, add the fish steaks, and fry for 10 minutes, turning every 2 minutes or so to make sure they brown evenly.

Transfer the fish to the prepared plate and let sit for 5 minutes to let excess oil drain, then transfer the fish to a large casserole dish with a lid.

Pour the marinade over the fish, cover, and refrigerate overnight. Taste, add more salt if needed, and serve chilled.

Chuletas a la Jardinera (Pork Chops with Garden Vegetables)

This one-pot dish is traditionally made with canned veggies, but using fresh ones makes it bright and surprisingly light. Serve over plain white rice.

Serves 6

6 bone-in, center-cut pork chops (about 3 pounds)

3 batches Adobo for Pork (page 11)

1 tablespoon olive oil

¼ cup Sofrito (page 10)

1 large onion, diced

2 medium carrots, diced

4½ cups peeled and diced tomatoes

1 large ear of corn, shucked, kernels cut off the cob

½ pound fresh green beans, ends trimmed and cut into 1-inch pieces

1 cup fresh or frozen green peas

Place the pork chops in a large bowl and pour the adobo over them, rubbing them well to fully incorporate it. Transfer the pork chops to a large zip-top bag or plastic container with a lid and marinate in the refrigerator for at least 30 minutes, or overnight if possible.

Heat the oil in a large, heavy-bottomed saucepan or Dutch oven over medium-high heat. Brown the pork chops well on both sides for 5 minutes total, then transfer to a plate.

Reduce the heat to medium and add the sofrito. Cook, stirring frequently, for about 5 minutes, until the mixture starts to brown and the liquid is mostly evaporated, then add the onion and carrots and cook for 5 minutes more, or until the onion start to turn golden. Add the diced tomatoes, scraping up any browned bits stuck to the bottom of the pot.

Return the pork chops to the pot and nestle them into the tomato sauce, spooning the sauce over them to cover. Bring to a simmer, then lower the heat, cover, and cook for 30 to 40 minutes, stirring lightly every 10 minutes to keep the sauce from burning, until the pork chops are tender and almost falling apart.

Transfer the pork chops to a clean plate and tent with foil. Add the corn, green beans, and peas to the sauce and cook for 5 minutes, or until the vegetables are cooked through but still crisp.

Serve the pork chops with the sauce and vegetables spooned on top.

Buñuelos de Viento en Almibar (Fried Doughnuts in Cinnamon Syrup)

These simple doughnuts in syrup were a staple in Tata's house. They can be eaten warm or chilled.

Makes 20 *buñuelos*

Syrup

3 cups sugar

4 cups water

1 cinnamon stick

½ teaspoon vanilla extract

½ teaspoon fresh lemon juice

Buñuelos

1 cup water

4 tablespoons (¼ cup) unsalted butter

½ teaspoon salt

1 cup all-purpose flour

4 large eggs

Canola oil for frying

Ground cinnamon for dusting

Make the syrup: In a medium saucepan, combine the sugar and water over medium-high heat and bring to a boil. Reduce the heat to a simmer, add the cinnamon stick, and cook, uncovered, for 8 to 10 minutes, until slightly thickened into a light syrup.

Add the vanilla and lemon juice and cover until ready to use.

Make the *buñuelos*: While you are cooking the syrup, combine the water, butter, and salt in a large saucepan and bring to a boil over medium-high heat. Remove from the heat, add the flour all at once, and mix with an electric hand mixer on low speed until combined.

Add the eggs one by one, mixing well until the dough is fully blended, thick, and sticky but not pasty.

Line a large plate with paper towels.

Heat 1½ to 2 inches of oil in a large, deep skillet or wok over medium-high heat until simmering. Drop a bit of dough in to see if it's ready—you'll know once the dough sizzles and rises to the surface.

Use two large tablespoons to scoop small balls of dough one by one into the hot oil (scoop with one and use the back of the other to drop the dough into the oil gently). The doughnuts will float to the surface of the oil.

Fry, turning the balls frequently, for 2 to 3 minutes, until they are evenly browned. Remove from the oil with a slotted spoon and place on the prepared plate to drain.

Arrange the *buñuelos* in a 9 by 9-inch casserole dish and pour the syrup over them. Serve dusted with cinnamon.

Pie de Limón
(Lemon Meringue Pie)

Tata was full of stories, but one that would have Mami and me in stitches was the story of the pie de limón. One day, Tata made this pie for a potluck. She was walking through the parking lot to her car, holding the pie up in her right hand like a waitress. Suddenly, a gust of wind came, lifted the pie, and it went *splat* against the nearest car windshield. Tata, in shock, put her hand down, turned, and kept walking. If I'd been there, I would have licked that pie right off that stranger's windshield, because this pie is *that* good.

Serves 8

Pie Crust and Filling

⅓ cup cornstarch

1 cup sugar

⅛ teaspoon salt

1½ cups water

½ cup fresh lemon juice

1 tablespoon lemon zest

4 large egg yolks

1 tablespoon unsalted butter

1 (9-inch) prepared piecrust, baked

Meringue

4 large egg whites

¼ teaspoon salt

½ cup sugar

Make the filling: Combine the cornstarch, sugar, and salt in a medium saucepan and whisk to incorporate.

Whisk in the water, lemon juice, and lemon zest, place over medium heat, and heat, stirring constantly, until the mixture just begins to boil and thicken. Remove from the heat.

In a small bowl, whisk the egg yolks, then quickly whisk the yolks into the hot filling.

Return the pot to medium heat and bring to a near-boil.

Add the butter and stir until fully melted and incorporated.

Preheat the oven to 400°F.

Make the meringue: In a large bowl, beat the egg whites and salt with an electric hand mixer on high speed until soft peaks start to form. Continue beating while slowly pouring in the sugar, and beat until firm peaks form.

To assemble: Pour the hot filling into the prepared piecrust, wiggling to spread the filling out evenly.

Using a rubber scraper, scrape the meringue out of the bowl and into the center of the pie and spread it out evenly to the edges of the crust.

Put the pie in the oven and bake for 7 to 10 minutes, until the meringue starts to turn golden brown, watching closely to make sure it doesn't get overly browned.

Remove from oven, place on a wire rack, and cool completely, about 1 hour. Refrigerate until cold and serve chilled.

Note: I hope the bakers out there will forgive my recommending the use of a premade piecrust. It's what Tata used, and I'm sticking as close as I can to the perfection she created.

Mami's Bizcocho de Ron (Mami's Rum Cake)

When my friends found out I was writing this cookbook, several asked if Mami's rum cake would be in it. And so it is. First I give you her original recipe, which uses a boxed cake mix. I highly recommend this recipe if you need to make something quickly and easily or aren't very comfortable baking. It's perfectly balanced and is my favorite cake to this day. But in homage to Mami, I've adapted her recipe to give it a little more depth, and that version follows. (In case you were wondering, my family calls me Bombi.)

Special thanks to chef, friend, and mentor Kathy Gunst for her help adapting this recipe.

Serves 6 to 10

MAMI'S RECIPE

Cake

Canola oil cooking spray

1 cup finely chopped walnuts

1 box butter-flavor cake mix

1 (3.4-ounce) box instant vanilla pudding mix

Unsalted butter

Eggs

¼ cup white rum

Rum Syrup

¼ cup (4 tablespoons) unsalted butter

1 cup light brown sugar

½ cup white rum

¼ cup water

Preheat the oven to 350°F. Grease a Bundt pan with cooking spray and sprinkle in the walnuts.

In a stand mixer fitted with the paddle attachment or a large bowl using a handheld electric mixer, combine the cake mix and pudding mix, then add the butter and eggs as directed by the instructions on the cake mix box. Add the rum. Beat at medium speed for 4 minutes.

Pour the batter into the prepared Bundt pan and level it with a spatula.

Bake for 33 to 35 minutes, until the cake is pale golden in color, slightly risen, and a toothpick or cake skewer comes out clean when poked in the center of the cake.

Remove from the oven and place on a wire rack to cool slightly.

Meanwhile, make the rum glaze: Combine all the glaze ingredients in a small saucepan and bring to a boil over high heat. Reduce the heat to medium-low and simmer for 5 to 7 minutes, until the sugar is fully

⫸⟶

dissolved and the glaze thickens just slightly.

While the cake is still warm, poke holes throughout the cake using the same toothpick or skewer you used to test the cake for doneness. Pour the hot glaze on top; don't worry if the cake doesn't take in the glaze immediately. It takes at least 10 minutes for the glaze to be absorbed.

Cover the pan with aluminum foil and allow to soak for at least 3 hours or overnight. Invert onto a plate, then slice and serve.

BOMBI'S RECIPE

Cake

Canola oil cooking spray

1 cup finely chopped walnuts

2 cups all-purpose flour

1 cup sugar

1 (3.4-ounce) box instant vanilla pudding mix

½ cup (1 stick) unsalted butter, cut into small pieces

2 teaspoons baking powder

1 teaspoon salt

½ cup milk

4 large eggs

½ cup coconut oil

½ cup white rum

2 teaspoons vanilla extract

Rum Syrup

½ cup (1 stick) unsalted butter

½ cup white rum

½ cup light brown sugar

¼ cup water

½ teaspoon vanilla extract

Preheat the oven to 325°F. Grease a Bundt pan with cooking spray and sprinkle in the walnuts.

In a stand mixer with the paddle attachment or a large bowl using an electric handheld mixer, combine the flour, sugar, pudding mix, butter, baking powder, and salt. Mix on medium speed for about 2 minutes, until fully incorporated.

Add the milk, eggs, and coconut oil and blend on low speed for about 2 more minutes, until smooth. Pour in the rum and vanilla and blend on low speed for about 1 more minute to form a thick batter.

Pour the batter into the prepared Bundt pan and level it with a spatula. Bake for 50 to 60 minutes, until the cake is pale golden in color, slightly risen, and a toothpick or cake skewer comes out clean when poked in the center of the cake.

Remove from the oven and place on a wire rack to cool slightly.

Meanwhile, make the rum glaze: Combine all the glaze ingredients in a small saucepan and bring to a boil over high heat. Reduce the heat to medium-low and simmer for 5 to 7 minutes, until the sugar is fully dissolved and the glaze is just slightly thickened.

While the cake is still warm, poke holes throughout the cake using the same toothpick or skewer you used to test the cake for doneness. Pour the hot glaze on top. Don't worry if the cake doesn't take in the glaze immediately; it takes at least 10 minutes for the glaze to be absorbed.

Cover the pan with aluminum foil and allow to soak for at least 3 hours or overnight. Invert onto a plate, slice, and serve.

Coquito (Coconut Eggnog)

Coquito is Puerto Rican coconut-y eggnog. We claim it as our own, but it's also beloved by Dominicans and Cubans. It's frothy and rich like a traditional eggnog, but it's made lighter by using coconut milk instead of heavy cream and swaps cinnamon for nutmeg and rum for bourbon or brandy.

It certainly was essential in my home over the holidays. Mami isn't much of a drinker, but she loves *coquito*. My dad was always the *coquito* master, and so this is an adaptation of his recipe.

Makes about 2 quarts

1¼ cups water

3 cinnamon sticks

8 large egg yolks

1 (13.5-ounce) can coconut milk

1 (14-ounce) can condensed milk

1 (15-ounce) can cream of coconut (Coco Lopez)

½ teaspoon vanilla extract

Pinch of salt

½ teaspoon lime zest

1 quart white rum, or to taste

Ground cinnamon

In a small saucepan, combine the water and cinnamon sticks. Bring to a boil over high heat, then reduce the heat and simmer while you prepare the remaining ingredients.

Pour the egg yolks into a large blender and blend on high speed for 3 minutes, or until they thicken into a cream.

Add the coconut milk and blend for 1 minute, then add the condensed milk and cream of coconut and blend for 3 minutes, or until thickened.

Remove the cinnamon sticks from the boiling water and reserve them. Pour the boiling water into the egg yolk mixture.

Add the vanilla, salt, and lime zest and pulse once to incorporate. Pour the contents of the blender into bottles or a pitcher.

Pour in the rum and the reserved cinnamon sticks and stir or swirl the bottles to mix well.

Refrigerate until fully cooled, then serve over ice in rocks glasses with a sprinkle of cinnamon.

> *Note*: This can get messy. It's important that you use a large blender, or, alternatively, cut the recipe in half if your blender can't fit this amount of liquid. Plan ahead by reserving a few liquor bottles for storing. A funnel is useful for helping transferring the *coquito* into containers.

2

Mofongo Blues

So while I didn't grow up *in* them, I grew up *of* the mountains, and all my life I have held that these connections are a beautiful and remarkable gift.

—Ronni Lundy, *Victuals*

My phone rang. I pulled it out of my back pocket and saw that it was Mami.

"You need to get to Utah by Thursday," she said, voice trembling.

It was a Sunday, and I was volunteering at a film screening in Manhattan. I was setting up the snack table when she called, and I immediately put down the small bag of Cheetos I was holding.

Tata died suddenly. Mami had just talked to her the night before and said that she sounded fine, maybe a little congested. But Tata's last years were difficult. She'd been diagnosed with Alzheimer's a decade earlier and struggled with dementia, at times seeing things that weren't there and often forgetting the names of her kids and grandkids. She also had been left blind in one eye and had such intense vertigo that she got sick every time she was in a car, no matter what speed you were going.

But the most difficult thing for her (and for me) was that she couldn't cook anymore. She couldn't chop, constantly burned things, and confused everyday herbs like culantro with oregano. One day she heated a whole can of soup in the microwave. And all she ever wanted to eat was hamburgers and cake. Though I didn't blame her; hamburgers and cake are delicious.

She'd celebrated her eightieth birthday just a month before, and I called her on Skype to sing her *feliz cumpleaños* (while my Tio Julin, who was her main caretaker to the end, flat-ironed her hair). He was the one who found her, sitting in her favorite brown velour recliner in her spotless apartment. She'd made her bed, was fully dressed with nails and hair done, teeth in. She was always so put together.

New York City is the worst place to feel sad. I headed home, and folks on the crowded sidewalks stared at my mascara-streaked face with more curiosity than concern. I bought a dozen red roses and a prayer candle from the Mexican grocery. Wrong virgin—Virgen de Guadalupe (Mexico), not Providencia (Puerto Rico)—but it was perfect, small and pink. I'd never lost a family member before, and I wasn't sure what to do. So I built a tiny altar with seashells, photographs, and a rhinestone butterfly broach I'd "borrowed" from her as a teenager.

I remembered the last meal I'd cooked for her—*chicharrón de pollo* (chicken nuggets), fried crisp like pork skins—and the memory made me hungry. As I sat, eyes puffy, my tissue pile steadily growing, all I wanted was something that tasted like home. Not like Puerto Rico, but like the home I'd claimed—the South. However cliché, that moment of extreme vulnerability made me want a bucket of fried chicken, mac and cheese, mashed potatoes with brown gravy, and coleslaw.

It seemed the most fitting meal, because both Tata and I had grown up half in the Caribbean, half in the South. I'd always believed that I was a lot like her, maybe because we'd both straddled the border between two worlds.

⁂

I was born in Rio Piedras, Puerto Rico, to twenty-year-old college students. My dad was studying computer programming, my mom decorating and design. They tried to find a way to pursue their studies and raise a tiny baby, but my dad ultimately went the

way of so many other young fathers with mouths to feed—he joined the Army.

My first home on the U.S. mainland was Fort Gillem, a small Army base just south of Atlanta, Georgia. Our neighborhood in suburban Forest Park was made up of identical brick townhouses with white doors and trim, with playgrounds of rusting metal and slides that burned your thighs in the summertime. I learned to swim (military-style) on that base, when Sergeant Swim Instructor threw me in the deep end and told me to get to the top. I also lost my first tooth there when I tripped and fell on metal bleachers during one of my dad's baseball games. It seemed everything on that base was made of metal.

We had a small Puerto Rican enclave there. The kids ran around past dark, rolling in our Fisher-Price cars and catching lightning bugs. Our families cooked out on the weekends, making *arroz con gandules* (rice with pigeon peas) and *costillas* (pork ribs) marinated in *adobo*. And although these events—where our parents danced salsa, drank rum, and spoke Spanish rapidly—were how they stayed connected to the island, my friends and I just ate our fill and began refusing to speak Spanish. In the summer the nights were hot just like Puerto Rico, and we would sit outside way past our bedtime waiting for our drunk parents to take us home, Kool-Aid smiles on our faces and high on sugar.

We ate mostly Puerto Rican food at home, so the first Southern foods I ever ate were in day care.

I remember my parents dropping me off one morning, half-asleep and grumpy, at the

La Petite day care in Mount Zion, Georgia. A teacher sat me down at a long table with a dozen other preschoolers and served me a plastic bowl of white, wiggly mush with an orangey-yellow cheese square melted on top.

I was six years old, the only Latina in my class. Like most kids, I ate simple things for breakfast—I was a connoisseur of Trix cereal and strawberry Quik at the time. I poked at the wiggle with the edge of my spoon to investigate. I frowned. A teacher noticed and exclaimed, "What? You don't like *guh-ree-its*?!"

"Nuh-uh!" I said, frowning and shaking my head.

"Well, you'll just have to go hungry, because that's what we got," she said, fist pressed firmly against her hip.

I surrendered and scooped a bit of the cheese square and mush out of the bowl, letting it slide off the spoon into my mouth. My disgusted expression brought on more giggles and snickers from teachers and other kids—many wondering aloud what on earth my parents fed me at home. Humiliated, I quit eating and went hungry that morning.

This was my first foray into (bad) Southern food. Then there were public school cafeterias, where I was forced to eat badly prepared lima beans, fried okra, baked beans, and peach cobbler. That's also where I ate foods like Frito pie and Mexican pizza (a kid once asked me if that's what my mom cooked, and I stuck my tongue out at him). Because at home, Mami never made anything remotely like these foods. Nothing was as offensive to her as collard greens, which she thought smelled like toilet. Cornbread was too dry, fried chicken too greasy, biscuits and gravy too *baboso* (snotlike).

My mother was a secret vegetarian. Growing up in Puerto Rico, Tata cooked everything from scratch with lots of love and lard. That meant Mami often came home from school to a giant beef tongue in the sink or a pot of stewed pigs' feet and garbanzos on the stove. All she wanted was fresh greens. Instead, she got vegetables stewed to smithereens in pig fat.

I realize now it wasn't just that Mami thought Southern food was nasty and smelly. This way of eating—the pigs' feet and smothered greens—were part of her past, and she wanted a better future for me. When things were good at home, Mami mostly fed us simple American foods like baked chicken and veggies—made Puerto Rican with *sazón* seasoning—or Puerto Rican foods such as *picadillo* made healthy by substituting ground turkey for beef. Her food was tasty, but part of me wanted something more.

You see, every once in a while the lunch ladies would get it right. I'd go through the lunch line and smile as I was served a pulled pork sandwich with pickles on a soft white bun and coleslaw that was still crunchy. I started to be able to tell the difference between those stale day care grits and food made with care.

So I got curious. Those same greens braised in broth and ham hocks, fluffy biscuits in peppery white gravy, yellow layer cake slathered in chocolate buttercream: these were dream foods. And in many ways more akin to the incredible foods I ate when I visited my grandmother in Puerto Rico. But because Mami didn't approve, they were out of reach. Except when I went to the home of Arica Slaughter, my childhood best friend.

The Slaughters lived in Rex, the next suburb over from us, in one of those nice neighborhoods with a name. It had houses with two-car garages, long driveways, brick mailboxes, and flowerbeds. Their house was in a cul-de-sac, and their yard stretched an acre, bordered by a small creek, a line of polleny pine trees, and a chain-link pen where Bosh—the Slaughters' Doberman—lived. The house had three bedrooms, a den, *and* a living room, and a kitchen with a giant sink, a double-wide stove, and one of those big refrigerators that opened like French doors.

Arica's mother, Miss Donna, was a skinny white lady from Tennessee with graying sandy blonde hair, a pointed face punctuated by a delicate nose, and bright blue eyes. She wore gold-rimmed bifocals and dressed in sweatpants, button-down men's collared shirts, and slip-on shoes.

Miss Donna spent her days watching daytime TV, smoking cigarettes, drinking gin and tonics, and cooking. She was fascinated that I'd never had foods that were everyday to her, like hoecakes with corn syrup, chitterlings with hot sauce, and black-eyed peas. Anytime she learned that I hadn't tried a certain food, she'd make it for me immediately.

Miss Donna never made me feel like an outsider. In Puerto Rico, grownups made me feel like my culture, my addiction to air-conditioning, and the way I spoke Spanish were signs that I was . . . different. And in the South, adults asked me questions like *What does your name mean? How spicy is your mom's cooking? Do your parents speak English?* These questions made me feel like I couldn't fit into their idea of "Latina," but I didn't quite belong in the South either.

Arica's house was a sanctuary, especially when my parents entered the throes of a divorce. They were either constantly fighting or my dad just wasn't around. But Miss Donna always greeted me at the sliding glass door with the biggest hug, clutching the back of my head and pulling me close to her chest.

When she called us in from the yard, where we were either digging something up or jumping on the trampoline, her cigarette-strained voice would crack.

"Aaarica, Von Marieee, time to eat!"

At Miss Donna's house, it was always time to eat. Her cabinets buckled with name-brand snacks—the kind my parents could never afford: Nabisco, Keebler, Lay's, Aunt Jemima, Kellogg's. She kept three extra freezers on the back porch, equally packed with steaks, roasts, whole chickens, gallons of milk—abundance in response to the profound poverty Arica's dad had grown up with.

Benjamin Slaughter, or Mr. Benny, was a six-foot-tall black man built like a football player, with a lazy eye he'd gotten after one of his brothers accidentally hit him in the back of the head with the end of a heavy baton. His eyeball had popped out of the socket, and his mom had pushed it back in with Vaseline. We all bear the scars and signs of childhood hurts and accidents. Mr. Benny's were just easier to see than some.

Some days I'd come in from playing outside, my hair full of pine straw from rolling down hills and shoes filthy from mucking around in the creek, and find Miss Donna sitting at the table staring at the wall, cigarette in hand, another gin and tonic in front of her in a rocks glass beaded with condensation.

"You alright, Miss Donna?" I'd ask.

She'd look over, sadly. "Yeah, baby. You hungry?"

She never went back to Tennessee after marrying Mr. Benny. She had been his secretary at the construction company he founded and ran despite his third-grade education. Benny worshipped Miss Donna, and Miss Donna adored him. He'd come in late from work, quiet and reserved, and in his deep, gentle voice, he'd say, "Good evening, Miss Donna." "Good evening Mr. Benny," she'd reply, looking back at him over the top of her glasses. I never saw them kiss or even embrace. But when Mr. Benny was home, he and Miss Donna sat side by side.

Miss Donna's father disowned her when she married Benny. A strong believer in the teachings of the Klan, he never forgave Donna for marrying a black man. Arica was born two months premature. Miss Donna said she was the size of a Barbie doll, small enough to fit in a shoebox. Arica had a half-sister, Stacey, who died in a car accident on a rainy morning two years after Arica was born. Stacey was twenty years old. Somewhere in her mind, Donna always wondered if her father had cursed her. After he passed away, she said she could feel his presence roaming the house, holding on strong to his hate but not able to let her go.

When I was twelve, Miss Donna had a heart attack and died suddenly of multiple organ failure. They suspected that her heavy drinking was to blame, that she might have also had colon cancer. It was my first funeral, and I went dressed in an oversized Tweety Bird T-shirt and black leggings.

"Are you sure you want to wear that?" Mami asked, one eyebrow raised.

I didn't know what else to wear. When I got there, I couldn't speak to Arica or Mr. Benny. I sat in the back with my mom and stared at Miss Donna's face peeking out of her casket. People hugged and cried, a pastor led the group in song. We left fifteen minutes later. Arica and I were never the same. I didn't comfort her as a friend should have. And I never went back to that house. Arica was my best friend, but it might have been Miss Donna I was visiting all along.

I think of her often: when I see a Doberman, or drink a gin and tonic, and especially when I make grits. I once told Miss Donna the story of the La Petite grits. She listened intently, brow furrowed, and quickly went to work to correct that bad memory. I watched as she warmed water and milk in a saucepan and slowly poured in white corn grits, stirring and simmering until they thickened and sputtered. She filled three bowls halfway and sat them down in front of me along with a jar of grape jelly (Arica's favorite), a stick of butter, a bowl of sugar, and salt and pepper.

I wish I could say that they were amazing, and that my obsession with grits started that day. Instead, we scooped three mostly uneaten bowls of grits into the trash. Perhaps it was the memory of those first grits still lingering on my palate. But Miss Donna didn't give up. Over time, we tried maple syrup, strawberry jam, Tabasco . . . and ultimately hit a sweet spot with cheddar cheese and lots of pepper.

Miss Donna seemed to understand that I needed to be coaxed and prodded, guided slowly, and given a chance to adjust my tastes to match my taste buds and my background. She helped me find my home in the South.

❧

Almost twenty-five years later, I traveled to Utah for Tata's funeral. It was only the second funeral I'd ever attended.

I was with my mom when she walked into Tata's apartment. To the right along the wall were six winter hats, each a different color and texture, hanging from white hooks on the wall—fluffy microfiber, fleece, knit wool, and brown faux fur.

I covered my face with my hands and let out a choked wail, feeling the hole left by her absence. I slowly pulled down all the hats. They made me think too much about her head . . . about her hair . . . I could see her pulling the edges down over her ears with frail, leather-skinned hands. She was always cold.

The apartment was as she'd left it: dishes put away, fridge filled with mango Powerade and vanilla Ensure, freezer bare except for an Asian frozen dinner and *chuletas* (pork chops) in Tupperware. Tata's bed was made, clothes folded and stacked.

I took a few things to keep: a Louis Vuitton purse, some necklaces made of large stones, a sweater that was surprisingly youthful, a white jacket with a real fur collar, a ceramic boxer dog figurine, an antique lemon press made for tiny *limones*, the ones she used in her famous *pie de limón*.

And as I started to clean, I unearthed evidence of her food obsession in every corner. Old *Bon Appétit* and *Better Homes and Gardens* magazines; cookbooks by Tata's favorite Puerto Rican chefs; folders filled with clippings from other American lifestyle magazines and from the food and wine sections of Puerto Rican newspapers like *El Nuevo Día*. Her archive went back decades.

I found handwritten recipes on the backs of to-do lists—some in the elegant cursive I remember growing up, others in the messy scrawl of Tata's later years. I even found a recipe for apple cake I'd sent her, also handwritten on lined white paper in what looked like my middle-school cursive.

I always knew my grandmother—like me—was obsessed with food. But I didn't know the extent of her love until I discovered the library of recipes tucked into her mattress and underwear drawer. In her last home, she kept two types of archives: family photos and cookbooks. And I knew then, as I'd always suspected, that she and I *were* deeply alike.

RECIPES

The recipes in this chapter are a combination of Puerto Rican dishes that strongly resemble Southern ones (such as fried chicken and stewed okra) and those that highlight the African roots of both the Caribbean and the South. You'll also find a few innovations that marry the signature flavors of the two regions.

Surullitos de Maíz (Fried Corn Cigars)

Mayo-Ketchup

Tomates Rellenos (Cherry Tomatoes Stuffed with Sardines and Anchovies)

Funche de Coco (Coconut Grits)

Coconut-Braised Collards

Plátanos Glacé al Horno (Oven-Glazed Plantains)

Quingombos Guisados (Stewed Okra)

Asopao de Pollo (Chicken and Rice Stew)

Pollo Frito (Fried Chicken)

Chicharrón de Pollo (Fried Chicken Nuggets)

Pastelón de Plátano (Sweet Plantain Shepherd's Pie)

Catfish, Corn, and White Bean Chowder

Salsa BBQ de Guayaba (Guava BBQ Sauce)

Pinchos de Pollo con Salsa BBQ de Guayaba
(Chicken Skewers with Guava BBQ Sauce)

Costillas de Cerde con Salsa BBQ de Guayaba
(Pork Ribs with Guava BBQ Sauce)

Besitos de Coco (Coconut Kisses)

Anticuado (Rum Old-Fashioned)

Surullitos de Maíz (Fried Corn Cigars)

Many Puerto Ricans I know claim this simple appetizer as their favorite. Maybe it's because it's basically deep-fried cheese grits dipped in mayo. Once my mom and I made them for a party at my uncle's house, and after putting together about two hundred, the plate slipped out of my mom's hands and crashed to the floor. The entire house gasped. When you make them you'll understand why the loss of them was such a tragedy that day.

Makes about 50 *surullitos*

2 cups water

1¼ teaspoons salt

1½ cups fine cornmeal

1 cup grated Edam, Gouda, or Parmesan cheese

Vegetable oil, corn oil, lard, or a mixture

Line a rimmed baking sheet with brown paper or paper towels.

Pour the water into a medium saucepan and add the salt. Bring to a boil, then remove from the heat and quickly whisk in the cornmeal using a fork. The mixture will quickly form into a dough.

Add the cheese and mix well with a fork. Immediately begin forming *surullitos* by scooping out a tablespoon of dough and rolling it into a ball, then rubbing the ball back and forth between your hands to form a cigar shape about 3 inches long. Work quickly, as the mixture becomes very unruly once it cools.

Pour oil and/or lard into a frying pan to a depth of 2 inches. Heat the oil over medium-high heat until just simmering. Test by dropping in a small piece of dough; it will sizzle and rise to the top when it's at the right temperature.

Working in small batches so you don't crowd the pan, fry the *surullitos* for about 4 minutes, moving them around in the oil with metal tongs as needed so they don't stick together, until they turn a deep golden color. As they are done, remove them from the oil one by one and drain on the prepared baking sheet. Serve immediately, or keep warm in a low oven until you are ready to serve.

Mayo-Ketchup

Mayo-ketchup is an obsession. It's critical for *surullitos* but is also great on *tostones*, sandwiches, french fries, or anything else you'd put mayo on.

Makes 1 cup

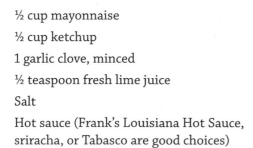

½ cup mayonnaise

½ cup ketchup

1 garlic clove, minced

½ teaspoon fresh lime juice

Salt

Hot sauce (Frank's Louisiana Hot Sauce, sriracha, or Tabasco are good choices)

Combine the mayonnaise, ketchup, garlic, and lime juice in a small bowl and whisk with a fork to incorporate. Season with salt and hot sauce. Cover and refrigerate until cold before serving.

Tomates Rellenos (Cherry Tomatoes Stuffed with Sardines and Anchovies)

This simple appetizer is the kind of thing my grandmother would have whipped up on the fly, having all the dry ingredients on hand at any given time.

Serves 8 to 10

4 cups cherry tomatoes, halved

1 (3.75-ounce) tin sardines in oil, finely chopped (oil discarded)

2 tablespoons finely chopped anchovies in oil (oil discarded)

20 pimento-stuffed manzanilla olives, finely chopped

1 garlic clove, minced

Freshly ground black pepper

Using a small spoon, carefully scoop out the seeds from the tomatoes into a bowl and reserve them. Place the tomato halves skin-side down on a large baking sheet.

Put the reserved tomato seeds into a fine-mesh sieve set over a small bowl and press with the back of a spoon to extract the juice.

In a large bowl, combine the sardines, anchovies, olives, garlic, and tomato juice and season with pepper. Mix well.

Carefully scoop sardine mixture into the tomato halves to just over the tops. Sprinkle with black pepper. Transfer to a serving plate and refrigerate until ready to serve. These are best enjoyed with your fingers on a warm, sunny patio.

Funche de Coco (Coconut Grits)

Ever since Miss Donna introduced me to a proper grit, I've become obsessed with them. There's nothing I wouldn't eat over grits and nothing I wouldn't put in them. They are, to me, a perfect food.

Funche is basically corn grits and was a dish served to enslaved indigenous and African people during Spanish colonization. It remained a common dish until the last century and was most often mixed with brown sugar and milk. Some food historians believe it went out of fashion because it became associated with blackness and poverty. Here's my take on a Southern (and once Puerto Rican) staple and a fusion of both cultures. Whenever possible, use fresh homemade coconut milk. It's wonderful topped with Coconut-Braised Collards (page 73).

Serves 4

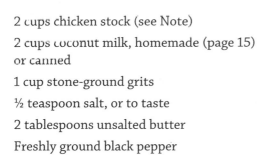

2 cups chicken stock (see Note)

2 cups coconut milk, homemade (page 15) or canned

1 cup stone-ground grits

½ teaspoon salt, or to taste

2 tablespoons unsalted butter

Freshly ground black pepper

In a medium-heavy saucepan or Dutch oven, combine the stock and coconut milk, then slowly whisk in the grits and salt until well incorporated.

Bring to a boil over medium-high heat, then reduce the heat to low. Cover and simmer, lifting the lid to whisk often, for 45 minutes to 1 hour, adding more water or stock as needed until the grits are creamy and thick.

Stir in the butter and season with pepper and more salt if needed.

Note: **You can easily substitute vegetable stock or water to make this dish vegetarian.**

Coconut-Braised Collards

Growing up, I was always served collards prepared the same way: some kind of pork and stock, with maybe a tomato, some onions, and always cooked until they were dark olive-green. I love collards and, like all other greens, want them to be a bright color and have some texture. This quick, simple recipe highlights that strong collard funkiness and tastes deceptively rich for a vegetarian dish.

Serves 4 as a side

1 large bunch collards, rinsed well in several changes of water

1 bunch scallions

1 tablespoon unsalted butter (optional; to make the recipe vegan, omit the butter and double the coconut oil)

1 tablespoon coconut oil

1½ cups coconut milk, fresh (page 15) or canned

1 tablespoon soy sauce

½ teaspoon salt, or to taste

Freshly ground black pepper

Cut off the bottoms of the collard stalks, then coarsely chop the leaves and stems and set aside.

Cut off the bottoms of the scallions, then thinly slice the whites and greens.

Melt the butter with the oil in a large wok or skillet over medium-high heat. Add the scallions and sauté for 1 minute.

Add greens and sauté for another minute, stirring well to incorporate, then add the coconut milk and soy sauce and bring to a simmer.

Lower the heat to medium-low and simmer, uncovered, stirring frequently, until the collards reach your desired doneness—7 to 10 minutes, or longer if you like your greens more tender. Season with salt and pepper and serve.

Plátanos Glacé al Horno (Oven-Glazed Plantains)

In my youth it was hard to find plantains in suburban Georgia, much less ripe ones. But on the special occasion when we did have them, I would beg Mami to make them caramelized in butter and brown sugar and dusted with cinnamon. We would eat them with rice and beans, the rich sweetness mixing with the savory meatiness of the beans. They are almost a dessert but pair perfectly with the most savory of Puerto Rican dishes.

Serves 6 to 8 as a side

Plantains

2 tablespoons salt

6 yellow plantains, peeled

6 tablespoons unsalted butter, cut into pieces

½ teaspoon ground cinnamon

Glaze

3 tablespoons unsalted butter

3 tablespoons dark brown sugar

Bring 2 quarts of water to a boil in a large saucepan. Add the salt and drop in the whole plantains one by one.

Boil with the lid off for 20 to 25 minutes, until they are easy to pierce with a knife but not mushy, then drain in a colander, taking care that the plantains don't break.

While the plantains are boiling, preheat the oven to 350°F. Place the plantains in a shallow baking dish side by side. Cut a long slit through the center of each and insert 1 tablespoon butter into each plantain. Put in the oven on the center rack and bake for 25 minutes.

While the plantains are baking, make the glaze: Melt the butter in a small saucepan over medium heat. Add the brown sugar and stir constantly until the sugar is fully dissolved. Cover and set aside.

Remove the plantains from oven and turn the broiler to low. Brush the plantains with the brown sugar glaze and return to the oven. Broil for 7 to 10 minutes, until they start to turn a dark brown color. I like to let them get a little burnt.

Remove from the oven and dust with the cinnamon.

> *Note:* When buying plantains for this dish, pick ones with deep yellow skins that have lots of black spots but are not entirely black, because it will make the finished dish too sweet.

> *Note:* They're best eaten the same day and tend to get hard when refrigerated.

Quingombos Guisados (Stewed Okra)

When I learned the Puerto Rican word for okra—*quingombó*—my first impression was that it sounded more African or indigenous than Spanish. This side dish is a nod to the influence of African ingredients and techniques in Puerto Rican and Southern cuisine. It's adapted from *Cocina Criolla* and is great served with sweet potatoes and pork or over Funche de Coco (page 71).

Serves 4 as a side

1 tablespoon olive oil

¼ cup Sofrito (page 10)

1½ cups diced tomatoes

1 bay leaf

1 pound okra, tops trimmed and sliced into 1-inch rounds

½ teaspoon salt, or to taste

1 cup water

Freshly ground black pepper

Heat the oil in a large, deep skillet over medium-high heat. Add the sofrito and cook for about 7 minutes, until the mixture begins to brown and the liquid is mostly evaporated, then add the tomatoes and bay leaf and cook for 1 more minute.

Add the okra, salt, and water. Bring to a boil, then reduce the heat and simmer for 10 to 15 minutes, until the okra begins to turn dark green and sauce is thickened. Season with more salt if needed and some pepper, and serve.

Asopao de Pollo
(Chicken and Rice Stew)

When we were really broke, Mami often made *asopao de pollo*, partly because it uses just a handful of ingredients that we always had on hand and partly because it was filling and deeply satisfying. It reminds me of Southern chicken and rice. This recipe can also easily be made with shrimp by substituting shrimp stock for the chicken stock and shrimp for the chicken and adjusting the cooking time for the shrimp to just a few minutes. Mami never made *asopao* with capers, olives, or peas, so I've listed them as optional.

Serves 6

1 cup basmati rice

1 tablespoon olive oil

¼ cup Sofrito (page 10)

1 large tomato, peeled and chopped

½ cup tomato sauce

2 bay leaves

6 fresh culantro leaves, finely chopped

1½ teaspoons salt

5 cups chicken stock

1½ pounds boneless chicken breasts, cut into ½-inch pieces

2 cups frozen or fresh green peas (optional)

1½ teaspoons capers in brine, drained (optional)

8 pimento-stuffed manzanilla olives (optional)

Cracked black pepper

Avocado slices

Rinse the rice in several changes of water and let soak while you prepare the remaining ingredients.

In a large saucepan, heat the oil over medium-high heat. Add the sofrito and cook for about 7 minutes, stirring frequently, until the mixture starts to darken and the liquid is mostly evaporated. Add the chopped tomato and tomato sauce and cook for another 5 minutes, or until thickened and slightly darkened.

Drain the rice, then add it to the pot along with the bay leaves, culantro, salt, and stock, stirring well. Bring to a boil, then lower the heat to low, cover the pot, and simmer for about 10 minutes, until the rice expands and the stew thickens.

Carefully remove the lid and add the chicken. Stir well, cover, and continue to cook for 7 more minutes, or until the chicken is cooked through.

Add the green peas, capers, and olives, if using, and stir well. Cook for another 3 minutes, then season with more salt if needed and some pepper. Serve with avocado slices.

Pollo Frito (Fried Chicken)

In her later years, Tata only got excited about a handful of foods. Among them were cake, hamburgers, and fried chicken. But who doesn't love fried chicken? When I'm old and gray I plan to demand it as well. This recipe is my take on a traditional Southern fried chicken recipe, but marinated overnight in *adobo*.

Serves 6

1 (3- to 5-pound) whole chicken, cut into 8 pieces

3 to 5 batches Adobo for Chicken (page 11)

1 cup all-purpose flour

1 tablespoon ground *achiote*

½ teaspoon onion powder

½ teaspoon salt

½ teaspoon ground black pepper

2 cups lard (see Note)

2 cups corn oil (see Note)

Put the chicken in a large bowl and pour on the adobo. Mix thoroughly with your hands to coat each piece evenly, making sure to get under the skin. Cover and let marinate in the refrigerator for at least 1 hour, or overnight.

Combine the flour, *achiote,* onion powder, salt, and pepper in a small bowl and stir to combine.

Put the chicken in a plastic bag and add the seasoned flour. Mix well to coat the chicken pieces evenly.

In a large, deep sauté pan or frying pan, combine the lard and oil and bring to a simmer over medium-high heat. To test the oil, sprinkle in a pinch of flour; it will sizzle once the oil is at the right temperature.

Meanwhile, line a large dish with paper towels and preheat the oven to 350°F. Set two wire racks over two rimmed baking sheets and set aside.

Working in batches, add the chicken pieces to the pan until full but not overcrowded. Fry the chicken for 7 to 10 minutes, turning once halfway through, until golden brown on the outside.

Transfer to the prepared dish as each batch is done. Once the chicken is properly drained, place it on the wire rack and bake for 15 minutes, or until the skin is well browned but not burnt.

Remove from oven and drain again on clean paper towels.

Note: You can use all lard or all vegetable oil if you prefer, but combining the oils gives the chicken a distinctly delicious porky flavor without being too heavy.

Chicharrón de Pollo (Fried Chicken Nuggets)

This was the last meal I cooked with Tata. She'd already forgotten so many of her cooking skills that I needed to walk her through each step, showing her how to squeeze a lime, explaining the difference between oregano and culantro. It was bittersweet, but the payoff—her face when she took the first bite—was worth it.

Serves 6

1 (3- to 5-pound) whole chicken

3 to 5 batches Adobo for Chicken (page 11)

¾ cup all-purpose flour

2 cups lard (see Note)

2 cups vegetable oil (see Note)

Fresh lemon juice

Salt (optional)

Hot sauce of choice

Using a sharp knife, cut the chicken into 2-inch chunks, leaving the meat on the bone. Rinse the chicken thoroughly with cold water to remove any bone shards, then dry well with clean paper towels. (Or get your butcher to chop it up for you.)

Put the chicken pieces in a large bowl and pour on the adobo. Mix thoroughly with your hands to coat each piece evenly, making sure to get under the skin. Cover and marinate in the refrigerator for at least 1 hour, or overnight.

Put the chicken in a plastic bag and add the flour. Mix well to coat the chicken pieces evenly. In a large, deep sauté pan or frying pan, combine the lard and vegetable oil. Place over medium-high heat and bring to 400°F.

Meanwhile, line a large dish with paper towels.

Working in batches, add the chicken pieces to the pan until full but not overcrowded. Fry the chicken for 7 to 10 minutes, turning once halfway through, until golden brown on the outside.

Remove the chicken from the pan and place on the prepared dish to drain excess oil. Let cool for a few minutes.

Sprinkle with lemon juice and salt if you like, and serve with hot sauce on the side.

Note: **You can use all lard or all vegetable oil if you prefer, but combining the oils gives the chicken a distinctly delicious porky flavor without being too heavy.**

Pastelón de Plátano (Sweet Plantain Shepherd's Pie)

Like a Puerto Rican version of a classic Irish shepherd's pie, this is some serious comfort food. It's sweet-savory at its best, with a subtle richness and briny acidity. It's also a quick weeknight meal and a great way to use leftover *picadillo*. When buying plantains for this dish, pick ones with deep yellow skins that have lots of black spots but are not entirely black, because it will make the *pastelón* too sweet.

Serves 6

2 tablespoons plus ½ teaspoon salt, or to taste

6 ripe plantains, peeled

4 tablespoons (¼ cup) unsalted butter, plus more for greasing and brushing across the top

3 tablespoons olive oil

3 to 4 cups Picadillo (page 36)

½ cup crumbled feta cheese, plus more for garnish (optional)

Bring 2 quarts of water to a boil in a large stockpot and add 2 tablespoons of the salt. Add the plantains one by one and boil for 15 minutes, or until easily pierced with a knife.

While the plantains are boiling, preheat the oven to 350°F. Grease a 9 by 9-inch casserole dish.

Drain the plantains, reserving ½ cup water from the pot, and place the plantains in a large bowl.

Mash the plantains with a potato masher, large fork, or wooden spoon. Using a

rubber scraper, fold in the butter, oil, reserved cooking water, and the remaining ½ teaspoon salt. Taste and adjust the salt accordingly.

Scoop half of the mashed plantains into the prepared dish and spread them evenly across the bottom of the pan.

Add the picadillo and spread out from the center, leaving at least a 1-inch gap from the edge of the pan. Sprinkle with the cheese, if using.

Add the remaining mashed plantain on top of picadillo, carefully spreading outward from the middle and making sure the picadillo doesn't break through.

Brush the top with a little melted butter, then place in the center of the oven and bake for 15 minutes, or until the top turns light golden brown. Remove from the oven and let rest for 5 minutes, then cut into squares. Sprinkle with additional cheese if you like, and serve with salad.

Catfish, Corn, and White Bean Chowder

I love catfish but have almost exclusively eaten it battered and deep-fried. This dish is a hybrid of a simple Southern fish chowder with Spanish white beans using Puerto Rican flavors. The funkiness of the catfish is balanced by the sweetness of the corn and the creaminess of the beans, and the shrimp stock kicks up the umami. You can substitute any other firm white fish, but if possible, stick to the bottom feeders. Note: After you chop the potato, keep it covered in water until you're ready to cook to keep it from browning.

Serves 6

3 quarts Shrimp Stock (page 13)

1 pound dried white beans, soaked in water to cover by a few inches overnight and drained

1 tablespoon olive oil

1 large onion, diced

4 large garlic cloves, minced

2 potatoes, peeled and cut into ½-inch cubes

1 tablespoon dried oregano

2 bay leaves

1 tablespoon salt, or to taste

1 pound boneless, skinless catfish fillets, cut into 1-inch pieces

2 ears of corn, shucked, kernels cut off the cob

1 teaspoon fresh lime juice

¼ cup chopped fresh flat-leaf parsley

5 fresh culantro leaves, finely chopped

Freshly ground black pepper

In a medium saucepan, combine the stock and beans. Place over high heat and bring to a boil. Reduce the heat to medium-low, cover, and simmer for 25 minutes, or until the beans are tender but not mushy.

In a large pot or Dutch oven, heat the oil over medium heat. Add the onions and cook for 2 minutes, or until they turn translucent, then add the garlic and cook for about 30 seconds, until fragrant. Add the potatoes and cook for 1 minute more to heat the potatoes through.

Add the beans and stock, the oregano, bay leaves, and salt. Increase the heat and bring to a boil, then lower the heat and simmer for about 7 minutes, until the stock is reduced and slightly thickened.

Add the catfish and corn and cook for 3 to 5 minutes, until the fish is solid white and no longer translucent.

Remove from the heat and add the lime juice, parsley, and culantro. Season with more salt if needed and some pepper, and serve with a crusty baguette or cornbread.

Salsa BBQ de Guayaba (Guava BBQ Sauce)

Dang, I love this BBQ sauce.

Makes about 2 cups

4 cups guava nectar

4 small guavas, quartered

2 garlic cloves

1 tablespoon Dijon mustard

1 tablespoon ketchup

1½ teaspoons red wine vinegar

Salt and freshly ground black pepper

Combine the guava nectar, guavas, and garlic in a medium saucepan. Place over medium-high heat and bring to a simmer. Reduce the heat to medium and simmer for about 20 minutes, until reduced and thickened. The sauce will darken slightly and have a glossy sheen. Strain through a fine-mesh sieve into a bowl, pressing on the fruit with the back of a large spoon to get the most out of the juice.

Whisk in the mustard, ketchup, and vinegar and season with salt and pepper. Set aside until ready to use with pinchos (recipe follows) or ribs, or store in an airtight container in the fridge for up to two weeks.

Pinchos de Pollo con Salsa BBQ de Guayaba (Chicken Skewers with Guava BBQ Sauce)

Driving through Puerto Rico, whether on interstates or in the cities, you'll often see signs for *pinchos,* or grilled meat skewers. Typically fatty pork or chicken thighs, they're cheap and often served *al ajillo* (with garlic) or with BBQ sauce, with a hunk of bread speared at the top of the skewer. My take is a little lighter and is a perfect contribution to a summer cookout. You will need 20 to 30 bamboo skewers for this recipe.

Makes 20 to 30 skewers

2 pounds boneless chicken breasts, cut into 1½-inch pieces

2 batches Adobo for Chicken (page 11)

2 cups Salsa BBQ de Guayaba (page 84)

Put the chicken in a large zip-top bag or plastic container and pour the adobo over it. Marinate in the refrigerator for at least 30 minutes, or overnight if possible.

Meanwhile, soak 20 to 30 bamboo skewers in a tall jar or container of water for at least 10 minutes to prevent them from burning on the grill.

Heat an outside gas grill, charcoal grill, or indoor grill pan to medium-high heat. Meanwhile, thread the chicken on the skewers until they are about three-quarters full with the pieces touching. Brush the chicken with BBQ sauce, then place on the grill or grill pan and cook, turning frequently and brushing with more BBQ sauce, for 7 to 8 minutes total, until the chicken is fully cooked through.

Remove from the grill, brush once more with BBQ sauce, and cover with foil until ready to eat. Serve with the remaining BBQ sauce on the side.

Costillas de Cerde con Salsa BBQ de Guayaba (Pork Ribs with Guava BBQ Sauce)

These are fall-off-the-bone, finger-lickin' addictive ribs. I made them once for Tata, and I swear she ate half a rack alone, wiping BBQ sauce off her face with the back of her hand, as did my pseudo-vegetarian mother. My advice: go ahead and double the recipe. You won't be sorry. Special thanks to Lisa Thrower for sharing her rib wisdom for this recipe.

Serves 4 as a main dish or 6 as an appetizer

1 ½ to 2 teaspoons smoked paprika

¾ to 1 teaspoon ground *achiote*

1 (3- to 4-pound) rack of pork ribs

3 to 4 batches Adobo for Pork (page 11)

2 cups Salsa BBQ de Guayaba (page 84)

Whisk the smoked paprika and achiote into the adobo. Place the ribs in a large shallow baking dish and pour the adobo over them. Cover with aluminum foil and marinate in the refrigerator for at least 30 minutes, or overnight if possible.

Place a rack in the center of the oven and preheat the oven to 300°F.

Place the marinated ribs in a new baking dish, cover tightly with foil, and bake for 3 hours, or until the ribs are evenly browned and a significant amount of fat has separated from the meat.

Remove from the oven, remove the foil, and transfer to an oven-safe wire rack set over a rimmed baking sheet.

Turn the broiler to low. Baste the ribs with BBQ sauce and place under the broiler. Broil for 7 to 10 minutes, watching closely to make sure the ribs don't burn, until crisp and browned on top.

Remove from the oven and let rest for 5 minutes. Cut into individual ribs, brush with BBQ sauce, and serve with remaining BBQ sauce.

Besitos de Coco (Coconut Kisses)

As a child, this was my absolute favorite dessert in Puerto Rico. The name means coconut kisses, and they're usually about the size of a tennis ball, caramelized and browned on the outside, soft and moist inside, typically with a halved maraschino cherry pressed into the top. These are smaller, simpler versions and not as sweet as the ones I had as a kid.

Makes 20 besitos

4 tablespoons (¼ cup) unsalted butter, softened, plus more for the cookie sheet

¾ cup dark brown sugar

4 large egg yolks

¼ teaspoon almond extract

¼ teaspoon salt

¼ cup all-purpose flour

3 cups packed sweetened shaved coconut flakes

1 teaspoon lime zest

Preheat the oven to 350°F. Butter a large cookie sheet.

In the bowl of an electric mixer, beat the butter and brown sugar on medium speed for 2 to 3 minutes, until smooth, creamy, and uniform in texture. One by one, add the egg yolks, then the almond extract. Add the salt, then slowly add the flour and beat until just incorporated, being careful not to overmix.

Fold in the coconut flakes and lime zest until fully combined and a thick batter is formed.

To form besitos, roll about 2 tablespoons of the mixture between your hands to form balls. Place them at least 1 inch apart on the prepared cookie sheet. Bake in the center of the oven for 30 minutes, checking at 20 minutes to make sure they don't burn on the bottom, until they are light golden brown in color.

Remove the sheet from the oven and transfer to a wire rack to cool.

Anticuado
(Rum Old-Fashioned)

I like my drinks dry and strong (I'm sure there's a joke there), and this is my take on a classic old-fashioned that is not too sweet and uses my favorite liquor, dark rum.

Makes 1 cocktail

1½ ounces aged dark rum

½ ounce rye whiskey

2 dashes angostura bitters

1 dash orange bitters

1 large orange peel twist

Combine the rum, whiskey, and bitters in a rocks glass. Stir well with a spoon to incorporate, cover with ice, and garnish with the orange twist.

3

Nosotras

To be a good cook I had to first envision the possibilities. I had to close my eyes and see and taste what was not there. I had to dream and discern it all on my tongue.

—MONIQUE TRUONG, *THE BOOK OF SALT*

I WAS BORN EATING, but I started cooking because I had to.

My family started falling apart when I was nine years old. Or at least that's when things got so bad that my dad, Papi, moved out. Afterward, Mami was under a mountain of debt and making just $35,000 a year while caring for two girls— ages ten and two— with little financial support from Papi. She worked nights and weekends, which made me largely responsible for feeding my sister, Kristina, and myself.

We lived in a rundown apartment complex in Morrow, Georgia, with rows and rows of identical ugly brick townhouses that re-sembled the military base that was my first home on the U.S. mainland. Most of the kids who lived there were black, with a sprin-kling of Latino families. The intersecting streets were riddled with speed bumps, and each Sunday a big yellow school bus would drive through, metal screeching as it lurched through our streets with candy tossed out like Willy Wonka to seduce the spawn of hedonist black and brown parents into the arms of the nearest Baptist church.

I was a nerdy kid on my way to becom-ing a nerdy teenager. I already wore glasses and had a mop of thick black hair that wasn't quite wavy or curly, and so it was just . . . frizzy. I typically got new clothes at the beginning of each school year: one, maybe two pairs of off-brand jeans, a few T-shirts and sweaters, and one pair of sneakers from Payless. The way I dressed was fiercely uncool in comparison to most of the kids in my neighborhood, as was my taste in music (at the time I played the violin and listened exclusively to classical music). As blossoming preteens, clothes and music were becoming the way we differentiated ourselves from one another.

But one thing we all had in common was the way we cared for our families. I had been put in charge of my sister. Parentified. At the playground, we looked out for each other's siblings; no one wanted a toddler falling off the monkey bars and busting their head open, because it meant none of us could play. Despite our differences, we were a community.

My parents' separation was followed by a steep nosedive in the quality and diversity of the food in my house. Powdered mac and cheese, chicken nuggets, spaghetti with jarred sauce, off-brand Beefaroni, off-brand American cheese singles, off-brand cereal in plastic bags, hot dogs, canned and frozen vegetables, and boxed mashed potatoes. Eggs, milk, orange juice, and red Kool-Aid. Rarely meat, mostly chicken. We ate so much poultry that my sister and I still have a strong aversion to leftover chicken.

We had a fifty-dollar biweekly grocery budget. But we never went hungry. Never. I took on the responsibility of feeding all of us, including Mami—who often went without dinner so Kristina and I had enough to eat our fill.

Then Mami got laid off. Only for a couple weeks, but we were already so strapped that she panicked—hard. She got two new jobs, one of them as an after-hours bank custodian. She rarely got home before 10 p.m., and I stayed up waiting for her. One night, I could tell by her face that she hadn't eaten all day. Her already pale skin was waxen and drawn, the circles under her eyes were dark as plums, and she looked . . . hollow.

"Mami, did you eat today?" I asked.

"No nena, pero no tengo hambre," she sighed, barely above a whisper, saying she wasn't hungry.

"Bueno déjame prepararte algo, tenemos espaghettis, o . . ." I insisted, telling her we had leftovers in the fridge.

"No, es que no tengo hambre, te dije," she said, a little irritated. She wasn't hungry.

"Mami, at least let me make you some mashed potatoes," I demanded sternly, giving her a look that must have signaled that I was serious. We'd done this dance before.

"Okay," she surrendered, and stood in the kitchen with me while I fixed her dinner. I put the potato flakes in a small white bowl with milk, water, a little garlic powder, and black pepper—a way I'd learned to doctor them up so they tasted less like cardboard. I put them in the microwave and, as I heated them up, rattled on about my day, what I'd learned at school, that I had done my homework, that I'd taken Kristina to the park after I picked her up from the sitter's.

She was there physically, but her mind was somewhere else. She would look at me, but almost through me. I know now it was because she'd reached such a level of sadness and exhaustion that she was struggling to escape.

The microwave beeped and I took out the potatoes as I had dozens of times before, stirring then tasting them to make sure they weren't too hot and had enough seasoning. I handed her the bowl, she took a bite and smiled weakly, but genuinely, and I knew that she was grateful. I kept talking, hoping to ease any anxiety she might have had that we were being left alone too often, or that the way I'd been tasked to care for our family—getting Kristina to and from the sitter, putting myself on the school bus every day, packing everyone's lunch, getting my homework done, and continuing to make good grades—I could handle it. It was my way of saying "Mami, I got you."

What I didn't know then is that this level of loss and hunger wasn't new to her, and that she'd first lived it when she was just slightly older than me.

·◆·

Tata was, without a doubt, an unusual cook. It seems growing up in Mississippi made her obsessed with vegetables, which she incorporated into much of her cooking. Brussels sprouts were her favorite, cooked with *sofrito*, or served with *chimichurri* sauce. Asparagus, green salads, green beans sautéed with *sofrito* and *jamón*, chayote squash battered and fried or diced and cooked with eggs. Sliced tomatoes with olive oil, salt, and pepper. Huge, freshly felled avocados from her tree in the backyard, lightly salted.

She subscribed to almost a dozen food magazines—*Better Homes and Gardens, Family Circle, McCall's,* and *Southern Living*—and spent an enormous amount of time trying to adapt those recipes to limited ingredients and Puerto Rico's tropical climate. She also received a weekly food encyclopedia in the mail sent in alphabetical segments. Apple, aspic. Balsamic, butter. Canapé, crème brûlée.

Mami's earliest memories are of Tata preparing farina (a kind of cream of wheat) for breakfast with brown sugar, butter, and cinnamon. Each day she would pick up Mami and Tío Julin from school at lunchtime and feed them *arroz montado de caballo* (white rice with a fried egg on top served with

ketchup), hamburgers stuffed with cheese, ham sandwiches, and leftovers. Whatever it was, it was homemade.

And each night she invented elaborate dinners. Giant "Fred Flintstone"–size steaks, whole roasted chickens, braised beef tongue, beef roast stuffed with chorizo, *pescado en escabeche* (white fish escabeche) served with rice or boiled yucca, and always a vegetable.

But this all changed when my grandfather left our family. His problems were many. Suffice to say he left one day and never came back and died in a prison somewhere far away.

My mother was fourteen at the time, and until then Tata had been a full-time homemaker. So she started working in a boutique, pulled my uncle out of the private Catholic school he'd gone to since he was five, and put him in public school. He was just old enough to get a job working as a grocery bagger and started working immediately. Mami stayed in private school but also started babysitting to help out. Much like me, out of necessity, she took over the kitchen, preparing simple dishes she could handle—spaghetti, rice and beans.

The transition was both tremendous and jarring. One week all Tata could afford was white rice and chickpeas, prepared simply with *sofrito*. After the sixth day of eating them—even though my uncle and mother didn't complain because they were so hungry (and it was still delicious)—my grandmother started to cry standing over a pot of rice in her kitchen.

Things got worse before they got better. The pain and stress of this time created a rupture that split the three of them apart, leading my mom to leave one day and move in with my father and his dad in Río Piedras, just outside of San Juan. And she was pregnant. And although my grandmother maintained her gourmet sensibility even when money was tight, my grandfather ate a steady diet of things fried in lard, spam, potted meat, doused in ketchup. If there was a vegetable, it was canned—typically peas and corn.

But once I was born, Mami dedicated herself to nourishing me the way she'd once been nourished, with homemade food. At six months old, she was already feeding me solid food (apparently I ate a lot), so she would stew whole chickens and root vegetables—yautía, ñame, yucca, or plantains—then blend them up and put them in a bottle outfitted with a nipple meant for a baby cow. *Slurrrrrp*, I would inhale the contents. It was easy and healthier than canned baby food or formula. She would also blend rice and beans and soups she'd made for her and Papi.

For most of my childhood, Mami did everything she could to feed me healthy, homemade food—just like her mother had done for her. And so when things got bad, I can only imagine what a blow it was. To be standing in her kitchen spooning chalky boxed mashed potatoes into her mouth with an expectant daughter looking up at her, much like she must have done when her own mother cried over a pot of garbanzos, wanting so badly to make things better in whatever way she could.

Food was always the measure of how well our family was doing. And it fluctuated many times because we were repeatedly

abandoned by the men who had pledged to be our partners and parents.

Cooking became a way for me to fix things. But after a while the monotony of our diet was maddening. Chopped-up hot dogs with melted American cheese and ketchup on Monday, spaghetti and jarred sauce on Tuesday, chicken nuggets and corn on Wednesday, leftover spaghetti on Thursday, *arroz con pollo* on Friday.

I started experimenting. I caramelized canned corn in butter and a bit of sugar, adding salt, pepper, and garlic powder to keep it savory. I sautéed onions, garlic, and herbs for our spaghetti sauce. I made dipping sauces for our chicken nuggets like mayo-ketchup or "BBQ sauce" made of ketchup, mustard, and garlic powder. For dessert I'd freeze orange juice in ice cube trays with toothpicks to make little ice pops.

Luckily, my sister, Kristina, was a really good eater. And I was deeply concerned that she eat well; I was her other mother. But I was a kid left alone with a kitchen full of odd ingredients and an interest in chemistry that to this day is purely culinary. So I tested recipes on her and watched her face expectantly. Sometimes it was a clear smile, her bright eyes and blonde curls bouncing, nodding. Sometimes she ate quietly, and I knew whatever adjustments I'd made were just okay.

Cooking for her was never a burden. She was my responsibility, and I took her happiness very seriously.

Once, when we were low on groceries and

I couldn't bear to repeat the food rotation, I pored through *Betty Crocker's Cookbook*—one of the few Mami had. There I found a recipe for fettuccine Alfredo—something I'd had once at Red Lobster on my birthday back when my dad was still around. The ingredients were simple: flour, butter, milk, Parmesan cheese—all of which we had Shaky Parmesan, not Parmigiano-Reggiano, and Kroger-brand spaghetti, not fettuccine. But I felt confident it would work.

Step by step I made a simple roux, poured in room-temperature milk, and stirred continuously, adding the shaky Parm. I dipped a spoon in to taste and felt for the first time that I had really, truly gotten something right.

But the white noodles and white sauce too closely resembled the boxed mashed potatoes that had become the mush of our situation. So I squeezed a few drops of blue food coloring into the pasta water, a few drops of green food coloring into the sauce. It looked like something dreamed up by Doctor Seuss, and when I served it to Kristina her eyes glistened with curiosity. She took a bite, and I knew that I had, in fact, gotten it right.

Food for us had become a ritual, a way of achieving normalcy. In my imagination, happy families ate meals together; mothers delighted in nourishing their children, making them smile with secret recipes they would pass on to their own kids. My role in preparing meals was equal to my sister's role in enjoying them. We engaged in an unknowing exchange, filling in the blanks left by my mother's absence while simultaneously holding a place at the table for her.

Good cooks need good eaters, and my first good eater was Kristina. She fostered in me an addiction to feeding people as a way of showing love. Cooking made me happy when I was otherwise deeply depressed, confused, and lousy with adolescent insecurity. I was moody, snappy, and cruel at times. But Kristina and I could count on sitting at our small dining room table every night, tablecloths, placemats, and napkins, a full set of silverware, glasses of water—and we would eat something I'd made with intention just for us.

RECIPES

This chapter features dishes that are largely invented, much like those I made for my sister when we were growing up. The recipes include heavy adaptations of classic recipes and others that came up as I began incorporating Puerto Rican flavors into my everyday meals. *Sofrito, adobo,* and *sazón* are incredibly versatile, and I hope this chapter will inspire you to use them often and add a little Puerto Rican flavor to *your* signature dishes.

Tostones Rellenos de Frijoles Negros y Salsa de Aguacate (Black Bean–Stuffed Tostones with Avocado Sauce)

Salsa de Aguacate (Creamy Avocado Sauce)

Culantro Pesto

PR Antipasto

Sopa de Plátanos Fritos (Fried Plantain Soup)

Boronia de Chayotes (Chayote Squash Hash)

Camarones a la Vinagretta (Shrimp in Citrus Vinaigrette)

Pollo en Agridulce (Sweet and Sour Chicken)

Pork Tenderloin Pernil Style

Conejo Estofado (Braised Rabbit)

Cazuela (Pumpkin, Sweet Potato, and Coconut Milk Custard)

Cascos de Guayaba (Guava Shells in Syrup)

Sofrito Bloody Mary

Rosé Sangria

Tostones Rellenos de Frijoles Negros y Salsa de Aguacate (Black Bean–Stuffed Tostones with Avocado Sauce)

Among the things I inherited from Tata after she passed away was a wooden tool for making *tostones rellenos* (stuffed *tostones*). *Tostones* are twice-fried green plantains that are smashed into disks. This recipe turns the fried, firm plantain disks into little cups you can fill with just about anything. Tata would often fill them with tuna fish mixed with capers, salt, and lemon juice. This simple, vegan recipe makes a versatile appetizer that anyone can enjoy.

Serves 4 as an appetizer

Tostones

Vegetable oil

3 green plantains, peeled and cut into 2-inch rounds

Salt

Black Beans

1 tablespoon olive oil

1 garlic clove, minced

1½ cups cooked black beans, drained and rinsed

1 teaspoon Sazón (page 12)

½ cup water

Salsa de Aguacate (recipe follows)

Diced tomato for garnish

Make the tostones: Line a large plate with paper towels and pour oil into a deep skillet or sauté pan to a depth of about 1½ inches.

Bring the oil to a simmer over medium-high heat. Test the oil by dropping a scrap of plantain in the oil. Once it sizzles, carefully add plantain rounds with a pair of tongs until the pan is full but not crowded.

Fry the plantains, flipping them every couple of minutes, until they're golden brown. Remove from the oil and drain on the prepared plate. Sprinkle lightly with salt and let cool while you fry the remaining plantain slices.

Put the plantain pieces into a *tostones rellenos* press. If you don't have one (likely), you can achieve similar results by putting the plantains one by one on a small plate and pressing them into a flat disk with the bottom of a coffee cup. Then place each pressed plantain round into a small ramekin and mash them in the middle with the bottom of a muddler or other round-ended kitchen tool.

While the plantains are frying, make the black beans: Heat the oil in a small saucepan over medium-high heat.

Add the garlic and sauté for 30 seconds, or until fragrant. Add the black beans, sazón, and water and bring to a simmer.

Reduce the heat to low and simmer, uncovered, for 7 to 10 minutes, until the sauce thickens.

Assemble the *tostones rellenos* by scooping the black beans into *tostones rellenos,* then topping with the creamy avocado sauce and diced tomato.

Salsa de Aguacate (Creamy Avocado Sauce)

This is an incredibly versatile sauce that is delicious on just about anything. Try it as a dipping sauce for Surullitos de Maíz (page 67) or on tacos.

Makes about 1 cup

1 ripe avocado, halved and pitted
1 garlic clove, minced
1 tablespoon fresh lime juice
¼ cup water, plus more as needed
Salt and freshly ground black pepper

Combine all the ingredients in a small food processor and process until smooth, adding more water as needed until the mixture is the consistency of yogurt or your desired thickness. Season with salt and pepper. Transfer to a bowl and serve immediately, or place in a container and refrigerate until you are ready to use it, though it should be eaten the same day.

Culantro Pesto

Almost every time I share a recipe that includes culantro, the recipient thinks it's a typo. It's also called *recao*, and it tastes strikingly like a blend between parsley and cilantro. I love it and have started to use it instead of cilantro in soups, stews, and braised meats. Here's my take on pesto using this versatile herb. It's great in chicken salad and on pizza or pasta.

Makes about 2 cups

2 garlic cloves

½ teaspoon salt, plus more to taste

Freshly ground black pepper

2 tablespoons pine nuts

2 tablespoons olive oil

1 cup packed fresh culantro leaves

⅓ cup grated Parmesan and/or Pecorino Romano cheese

Combine the garlic, salt, pepper to taste, and pine nuts in a food processor. Add the oil and culantro and process until smooth. Add the cheese and pulse to incorporate. Store in an airtight container until ready to use, up to 1 week in the refrigerator or 4 months in the freezer.

PR Antipasto

Whenever folks would show up to Tata's house, she always had something
to snack on—a hunk of cheese, some guava paste, salami, Ritz crackers,
or chips. Over the years, like any good host, I've adopted this same cus-
tom. Here is my take on a classic Italian antipasto plate, but with Puerto
Rican staples. These are my favorite ingredients, but you can mix and
match based on what you like or have available, or add your own ingredients. But the guava and cheese might become your next obsession.

Amount varies

Guava paste, cut into thin slices

Queso de hoja or *queso fresco*, sliced

Spanish chorizo, thinly sliced

Salami or *soppressata*, thinly sliced

Castelvetrano olives

Large pimento-stuffed manzanilla olives

Aged Manchego cheese

Galletas export soda or saltine crackers

Italian baguette, cut into medium-thin
rounds

Arrange everything on a large wooden board
with knives for cutting the cheese and guava
paste.

Sopa de Plátanos Fritos (Fried Plantain Soup)

This simple pureed soup is incredibly rich and dynamic. It's great as a starter garnished with tomatoes and *cotija* cheese, or if you want to make a meal out of it, add a few large handfuls of baby spinach and up the garnish.

Serves 6 as starter or 8 as a main dish

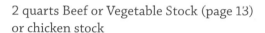

2 quarts Beef or Vegetable Stock (page 13) or chicken stock

4 green plantains

Vegetable oil and lard for frying (lard is optional but delicious)

Juice of 2 lemons

Salt and freshly ground black pepper

1 tomato, diced

2 tablespoons finely chopped fresh cilantro stems

½ cup grated Parmesan or *cotija* cheese

Bring the stock to a boil in a large stockpot over high heat, then reduce the heat to low and simmer while you prepare the plantains.

To peel the plantains, cut off the ends, then make three lengthwise slices through the skin. Carefully pull up the peel, starting at one of the corners, then cut the plantains into 1½-inch rounds. Watch out—plantain skins will stain your hands and clothing.

Heat the oil and/or lard over medium-high heat. Drop in a tiny piece of plantain to test the oil; it will sizzle once the oil is ready. Line a large plate with paper towels to drain the plantains. Fry the plantains in batches, turning several times, until golden brown, about 5 minutes per batch. Using a slotted spoon, remove the plantains from the oil and drain on the prepared plate while you fry the rest.

Place the plantains in a bowl and mash them with a large wooden spoon or potato masher. Add to the broth and use an immersion blender to blend until smooth, or blend in batches in a standard blender.

Add the lemon juice and season with salt and pepper. Spoon into bowls and serve garnished with diced tomato, cilantro, and cheese.

Boronia de Chayotes (Chayote Squash Hash)

This is a homey, quick vegetarian dish that's great for brunch or dinner. It's very versatile and is good with sausage, feta cheese, chopped broccoli, or spinach.

Serves 4

1½ teaspoons salt, plus more to taste

3 large chayotes

3 large eggs

1 tablespoon olive oil

6 tablespoons Sofrito (page 10)

1 cup diced tomatoes

Freshly ground black pepper

Pour 2 quarts of water into a large saucepan and bring to a boil over high heat. Add 1 teaspoon of the salt. Have a bowl of ice water ready.

Cut the chayotes in half and remove the seeds. Add the chayotes to the boiling water one by one and boil for 25 minutes, or until the skins become pale green and the flesh is easily pierced with a fork.

One by one, carefully remove the chayotes from the boiling water to the ice water, then drain.

Cut the chayotes into ½-inch cubes and transfer to a large bowl. In a separate bowl, beat the eggs.

Heat the oil in a medium saucepan over medium-high heat. Add the sofrito and cook for 7 minutes, or until it starts to brown and the liquid is mostly evaporated. Add the tomatoes and cook for 1 more minute to form a thick sauce.

Add the chayotes and cook, stirring frequently, for 5 more minutes, or until the chayotes are fully tender and the sofrito is well incorporated.

Pour in the beaten eggs and the remaining ½ teaspoon salt and stir continuously with a wooden spoon for 3 minutes, or until the eggs are set. Season with salt and pepper and serve immediately.

Camarones a la Vinagretta (Shrimp in Citrus Vinaigrette)

My parents gave me my first shrimp to peel when I was five years old, and I had a real knack for it. This simple recipe pairs tender shrimp with bright herbs, crisp citrus fruits, and creamy avocado. It's great to make ahead of time, though be sure to save the avocado until you are ready to serve. These *camarones* make for a great light dinner or an appetizer or lunch served over mixed greens or butter lettuce.

Serves 4

Vinaigrette

2 plum tomatoes, diced

3 tablespoons fresh citrus juice (lemon, lime, orange, grapefruit, or a combination)

2 tablespoons extra virgin olive oil

⅛ teaspoon Dijon mustard

1 tablespoon chopped fresh oregano or thyme

1 tablespoon chopped fresh cilantro

1½ teaspoons chopped fresh culantro

Salt and freshly ground black pepper

Poached Shrimp

1 quart water

3 tablespoons kosher salt, plus more to taste

4 peppercorns

2 bay leaves

1 pound shrimp, peeled and deveined

1 avocado, peeled, pitted, and coarsely chopped

Make the vinaigrette: Combine the tomatoes, citrus juice, oil, mustard, oregano, cilantro, and culantro in a large bowl. Season with salt and pepper.

Poach the shrimp: In a large saucepan with a lid, combine the water, 1 tablespoon of the salt, the peppercorns, and bay leaves and bring to a boil over high heat. While the water is coming to a boil, prepare an ice bath by emptying a tray of ice cubes into a large bowl and adding the remaining 2 tablespoons salt and enough water to cover.

Add the shrimp to the boiling water, turn off the heat, cover, and let sit for 1 to 2 minutes.

Drain the shrimp in a colander, then transfer to the ice bath. Stir well and let sit until fully cooled, about 5 minutes.

Drain the shrimp thoroughly, shaking the strainer and dabbing the shrimp with a clean paper towel to remove excess water.

Add the shrimp to the bowl with vinaigrette and toss to incorporate. Add the chopped avocado, taste, and add salt and pepper if needed. Serve immediately.

Pollo en Agridulce
(Sweet and Sour Chicken)

I didn't eat anything like this growing up but was immediately drawn to it when I started cooking my way through Tata's copy of *Cocina Criolla*. I've adapted the recipe to make it lighter and adjusted the cook time to keep the chicken from drying out. It's an excellent one-pot dish that can be made on a weeknight with few ingredients. Serve it over Funche de Coco (page 71) with Coconut-Braised Collards (page 73) or a simple salad.

Serves 6

1 (3- to 4-pound) whole chicken

3 to 4 batches Adobo for Chicken (page 11)

2 tablespoons unsalted butter

½ cup dark brown sugar

¼ cup red wine vinegar

3 small Spanish chorizos

Rinse the chicken and pat dry with paper towels.

Season the chicken with the adobo and let marinate for 30 minutes on the counter or up to overnight in the refrigerator.

In a large, heavy-bottomed saucepan or Dutch oven, melt the butter over medium-high heat. Add the chicken to the pot breast-side down and sear until well browned on the bottom, 3 to 5 minutes, then turn and sear until browned on the second side, about another 3 to 5 minutes.

Using tongs, transfer the chicken to a plate, then lower the heat to medium and add the brown sugar, vinegar, and chorizos. Cook,

stirring frequently, for 3 to 5 minutes, until the brown sugar is melted. Return the chicken to pot breast-side down and nestle the chorizos around it.

Cover, reduce the heat to low, and cook for 30 minutes, or until the breast is evenly browned. Rotate the chicken by inserting tongs into the chicken's cavity and flipping it over so it's breast-side up. Cook for an additional 30 to 40 minutes, until the chicken is fully cooked through and a meat thermometer inserted into the deepest part of the thigh registers 185°F and the breast registers 165°F.

Remove the chicken from the pan to a carving board and let rest for 5 minutes. Pour any accumulated juices into the remaining sauce in the pan.

Remove the chorizos and slice them thinly. Strain the sauce through a fine-mesh sieve into a serving bowl.

Carve the chicken and serve with the sliced chorizos and sauce.

Pork Tenderloin Pernil Style

Mami has always had an aversion to fat. Growing up, she never made anything with *tocino* (fatback), and fed us only lean meats. Pernil is about as traditional as you can get in Puerto Rico. It's a pork shoulder marinated overnight in *adobo*, then slow roasted like you would a Southern pork shoulder. It's succulent, and I love it. But this adaptation, inspired by Mami, achieves the same flavor and succulence in a quicker, leaner dish.

Serves 6

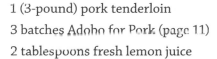

1 (3-pound) pork tenderloin

3 batches Adobo for Pork (page 11)

2 tablespoons fresh lemon juice

Cut a series of deep holes throughout the tenderloin and rub it down with the adobo, pushing the seasoning into the holes. Let marinate for 30 minutes on the counter or up to overnight in the refrigerator.

Meanwhile, preheat the oven to 400°F. Line a rimmed baking pan with foil.

Place the tenderloin in the center of the pan and put it in the center rack of the oven. Bake for 30 minutes, flipping every 10 minutes until evenly browned.

Remove from the oven and set the tenderloin on a carving board to rest.

Pour the lemon juice into the baking pan and carefully mix it into the pork juices, scraping up any browned bits. Pour the pan sauce into a small bowl and adjust the seasonings to taste.

Cut the pork into 1-inch slices and transfer to a serving dish. Serve with reserved pan juices.

Conejo Estofado (Braised Rabbit)

Rabbits aren't commonly thought of among Puerto Rican dishes, but they've long run wild and have also been farmed as livestock on the island. Rabbit is often stewed with *sofrito* and root vegetables and served over rice, particularly in rural parts of the island. Growing up, my mother never cooked anything this decadent, nor did we have easy access to rabbit in suburban Georgia. But it has become one of my favorite dishes. Try it served over rice or Funche de Coco (page 71).

Serves 6

2 (2- to 3-pound) rabbits, cut into 6 pieces each

1 (8-ounce) can tomato sauce

1 tablespoon salt, plus more to taste

¼ teaspoon cracked black pepper

⅓ cup olive oil

¼ cup red wine vinegar

2 teaspoons sweet paprika

1 tablespoon Sazón (page 12)

10 garlic cloves, minced

1 yellow onion, finely chopped

1 cup dry white wine

¼ cup pimento-stuffed manzanilla olives

¼ cup capers in brine, drained

¼ cup finely chopped roasted red bell pepper

1 pound white potatoes, peeled and sliced into 1-inch rounds

Rinse the rabbit pieces well and dry thoroughly with paper towels. Place the rabbit pieces in a large, heavy-bottomed saucepan or Dutch oven.

Combine the tomato sauce, salt, pepper, oil, vinegar, paprika, sazón, garlic, and onion in a medium bowl and whisk together. Pour the mixture over the rabbit.

Place the pan over high heat and bring to a boil. Reduce the heat to low, cover, and simmer, stirring occasionally, for 45 minutes.

Add the wine, olives, capers, and red pepper, then layer on the potato slices in a circle with the slices overlapping. Raise the heat to medium-high, return to a boil, then cover, reduce the heat to low, and simmer for 30 minutes, or until the rabbit is tender and falls easily off the bone.

Remove the rabbit pieces from the pan to a plate and let cool slightly. Continue to simmer the potatoes in the sauce for another 10 minutes to thicken it slightly.

Meanwhile, carefully pull the rabbit meat from the bones and fold the meat into the sauce. Divide among plates and serve.

Cazuela (Pumpkin, Sweet Potato, and Coconut Milk Custard)

Silky smooth with autumn flavors, this dessert is decadent without being overly rich. It can be eaten warm just out of the oven or chilled with whipped cream and any of the other toppings suggested below.

Serves 10

4 tablespoons (¼ cup) unsalted butter, softened

2¼ teaspoons salt

1½ pounds *calabaza* (pumpkin), peeled and chopped

1½ pounds white sweet potatoes (Korean or Dominican), peeled and chopped

1 (3-inch) piece fresh ginger, chopped

1 cinnamon stick

1 star anise pod

8 whole cloves

3 large eggs

¾ cup coconut milk, fresh (page 15) or canned

1 cup light brown sugar

3 tablespoons all-purpose flour

Optional toppings: lightly sweetened whipped cream, toasted grated coconut, dark chocolate shavings

Grease 10 (8-ounce) ramekins with 1 tablespoon of the softened butter and arrange on a rimmed baking sheet.

Bring 2 quarts of water to a boil over high heat. Add 1½ teaspoons of the salt. Add the pumpkin and sweet potatoes and boil until soft, 25 to 30 minutes. Drain and transfer to a large bowl.

In a small saucepan, combine the ginger, cinnamon stick, star anise, and cloves with ¼ cup water. Bring to a boil over medium-high heat and boil for 5 minutes. Strain the water into a bowl and set aside.

Preheat the oven to 400°F.

Using an electric mixer, blend the pumpkin, sweet potatoes, and the remaining 3 tablespoons butter on medium speed until smooth, about 3 minutes. Add the eggs, coconut milk, brown sugar, the remaining ¾ teaspoon salt, the flour, and the reserved spice water and blend for 1 more minute, or until smooth.

Pour the mixture into the prepared ramekins and bake for 30 to 40 minutes, until the custard is no longer wiggly and the tops are golden brown.

Remove from the oven and place on a wire rack to cool fully. Cover the ramekins with plastic wrap and chill in the refrigerator. Top with whipped cream and toasted coconut and/or dark chocolate shavings if you like.

Cascos de Guayaba
(Guava Shells in Syrup)

Fresh guavas can be incredibly hard to find. Unfortunately, I don't have any advice other than if you see them, buy a lot of them and make this dessert.

Serves 6

3 pounds ripe guavas

7 cups water

3 cups sugar

2 tablespoons fresh lemon juice

½ pound *queso de hoja, queso fresco,* or other soft, mild white cheese

Zest of 1 orange

Wash and peel the guavas using a sharp knife or vegetable peeler, then cut them in half.

Using a small spoon, scoop out the seeds. Reserve the seeds and pulp to infuse with alcohol or make syrup or Salsa BBQ de Guayaba (page 84).

Pour the water into a large saucepan and add the guava shells, skin-side down. Bring to a boil over high heat, then reduce the heat to medium-high and simmer, uncovered, for 25 minutes without stirring.

Add the sugar and continue to simmer, uncovered, for about 1 hour without stirring, until the guavas are tender but not falling apart, testing after 45 minutes to make sure they don't get too soft.

Remove from the heat and add the lemon juice. Let the shells cool, then transfer them and their syrup into a large container, cover, and refrigerate until cold. Divide the guava shells among bowls, pour the syrup over them, and serve with a large slice of queso fresco. Garnish with orange zest.

Sofrito Bloody Mary

This is just damn delicious. The *sofrito* for this cocktail is made with green onion to give it a more complex flavor; if you have some left over from your cocktails (good luck), you can cook with it just the same as any other *sofrito*.

Special thanks to Marisa Cadena, who helped design this recipe based on her own award-winning Bloody Mary recipe.

Makes 4 cocktails

Sofrito

½ red bell pepper, seeded and coarsely chopped

2 *ají dulce* chiles, seeded

4 garlic cloves, peeled

1 bunch scallions, whites only, coarsely chopped

8 fresh culantro leaves

4 fresh cilantro sprigs, chopped

Bloody Mary Mix

4 tablespoons fresh lime juice

2 tablespoons Worcestershire sauce

¼ cup soy sauce

4 cups tomato juice

¼ cup Valentina hot sauce or another hot sauce

Pinch of salt

Cracked black pepper

6 ounces gin or vodka

Garnishes: fresh culantro leaves, pimento-stuffed manzanilla olives, lime slices, and/or a Sazón (page 12) salt rim

Make the sofrito: In a small food processor, blend the sofrito ingredients starting with bell pepper, *ají dulce* chiles, and garlic, then adding the scallions, culantro, and, last, the cilantro sprigs and blend into a smooth paste.

Make the Bloody Mary mix: Combine the lime juice, Worcestershire sauce, soy sauce, tomato juice, hot sauce, salt, and pepper in a medium pitcher and mix well to incorporate.

Spoon 1 tablespoon sofrito into individual tall glasses, add 1½ ounces gin or vodka to each glass, and stir well.

Fill each glass with ice, then pour in the Bloody Mary mix. Garnish with culantro leaves, manzanilla olives, lime slices, and/or a sazón salt rim.

Rosé Sangria

This summery, tropical cocktail is as pretty as it is delicious. Don't skimp on the passion fruit—it really makes the drink sparkle.

Makes 6 glasses

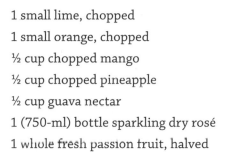

1 small lime, chopped

1 small orange, chopped

½ cup chopped mango

½ cup chopped pineapple

½ cup guava nectar

1 (750-ml) bottle sparkling dry rosé

1 whole fresh passion fruit, halved

Combine all the ingredients except the passion fruit in a large pitcher and stir well to incorporate.

Pour over ice and garnish each glass with a teaspoon or so of the passion fruit pulp.

4

Retorno

Lo malo de llorar cuando uno pica cebolla no es el simple hecho de llorar, sino que a veces uno empieza, como quien dice, se pica, y ya no puede parar.

The trouble with crying over an onion is that once the chopping gets you started and the tears begin to well up, the next thing you know you just can't stop.

—Laura Esquivel, *Como Agua Para Chocolate (Like Water for Chocolate)*

WHEN I WAS TWENTY-THREE YEARS OLD, just before Thanksgiving, Tata had the heart attack and stroke that may have triggered her Alzheimer's. She was at work and collapsed at her desk. Afterward she was in a coma for a week. Because she only had one kidney and high blood pressure and had lived a helluva life, we weren't surprised. But it was sudden.

One night while she was still in a coma, I was in her hospital room and suddenly heard the sound of her voice reciting a Rubén Darío poem, as she had throughout my childhood. *Verso, perla, pluma, y flor.* A verse, a pearl, a feather, and a flower.

She woke up the next morning.

We all knew her as an unshakeable survivor. We thought this was just one more hurdle. It wasn't. She never bounced back. We soon learned she was experiencing dementia and would never be able to take care of herself again. She moved to Atlanta to live with my mother, severing my tether to the island. Or fraying it, at least.

It was eleven years before I went back to Puerto Rico, and I returned with my husband. He and I had met in a bar nine years before. And we fell in love, hard.

Our faces fit. When we kissed, our noses smooshed together; we held hands immediately and touched constantly. And we walked down the street as one, connected like those little fish that live on sharks.

Early on I learned he had a major flaw. He was . . . vegan. And I decidedly loved meat. All meats. The first time I cooked for him, I felt compelled to make something from my homeland, but at that time I was only familiar with the porkiest, most fried forms of the island's cuisine. I called my mom, we talked, and I settled on white rice with chickpeas stewed in *sofrito* and tomatoes, yucca with *mojo caliente*—like Tata used to make—*plátanos maduros* (sweet plantains), and sliced avocado.

He'd never tasted anything like it and ate with a gusto that mirrored my sister Kristina's when she was kid. He was the first partner I ever cooked for. We both ate so much we were too full to have sex. We slept like bears, cuddling content with the heaviness of rice and root vegetables and food prepared with love.

We were young, but it didn't matter. We knew it was forever, and seven years later we got married on a cliff in Northern California, on the edge of the world, fingers enlaced, staring off into the endless Pacific Ocean toward our future.

Although we were together before Tata died, he never really knew her. Her Alzheimer's had set in deep by the time he came around. She never recognized him or even remembered that I was married. Still, she was always sweet to him.

After her funeral, I knew I needed to go back to the island. So we took a weeklong vacation. I wanted to be where Tata had been when she was still herself and remember her when she was her happiest and most vibrant. I wanted to say good-bye to her there.

In her honor, we ate our way across the island: seafood-stuffed *mofongo*, *léchon asado*, *quesitos*, *pastelitos de guayaba*, *mallorcas con jamón y queso*, *salmorejo*, shark *pinchos*, and small, sweet oysters. We also crawled through caves, kayaked the bioluminescent bay by moonlight, and got food poisoning from an octopus salad. We recovered by lying on the beach in Fajardo all day drinking water under a Coccoloba tree. It was magical.

Or so it seemed. In reality we were already falling apart. On that same trip we visited a lighthouse on the southwest coast. We tried to park our rental car and, as usual, people were acting crazy—taking up multiple spaces, parking slightly askew, shouting insults at each other in Spanish. It was very Puerto Rican. It didn't bother me at all because I knew we just needed to be patient until folks got sorted out. But I didn't say that out loud, and I didn't realize it was making him very upset. He took my lack of communication as disinterest in his stress, as a deliberate affront to his feelings, and he raised his voice at me. And then we didn't talk for an hour, in the most beautiful place I've ever been. He seemed to feel everything I did was against him. And I was so terrified of what was happening that I just looked off into the distance.

We'd started drifting apart more than a year before. I'd hoped our vacation would be a moment of coming together, an opportunity to smooth over the tensions that we couldn't seem to shake. But it wasn't that. And when we came home, our relationship unraveled at an accelerated pace. I became increasingly depressed and hid it from everyone. I had seen my mother and my best friend through separations, but no one can tell you how to do it yourself. I had to walk alone across hot coals, burning the skin off the bottoms of my feet. I had to hit a brick wall going 100 miles per hour.

I lost my appetite a couple months before our relationship officially ended. But I didn't even realize I wasn't eating until I called my best friend, Sarah, and jokingly said that I couldn't remember the last time I'd chopped an onion.

"What do you mean?" she asked. I could tell she was disturbed.

"I just really can't remember the last thing I cooked . . . ," I replied, half laughing, trailing off.

Come to think of it, in those last two months of marriage I could only remember cooking three meals, all of them soups. I was rapidly losing weight. In a search for clothes that would fit, I tried on a pair of pants that were skintight even when I was at my thinnest, right before our wedding. They hung off my hips.

Six months after our trip to Puerto Rico, we split up. It felt like cutting off my right arm. Like a death. Like I was a child lost in the basement of my own house. It was all those things and more. Mostly nothing made sense, and every day felt like an eternity filled with a kind of pain that extended from the tips of my toes to the top of my head and across every inch of my skin.

I had loved him like I loved food, like I loved eating. He was essential, like the glass of water you bring to bed at night whether you drink it or not. Hot coffee in the morning, consistent and beautiful and aromatic and necessary; a ritual that tells you your day's begun. And so when he was gone I didn't care about my body anymore and quit eating. The shock of that starvation was tremendous, because I'd always been a binge eater. Before then, when I was sad, I gorged to eat my pain away. When I was a kid and we had nothing but processed foods, I still overate. Two cans of green peas

or a twelve-egg omelet with twelve slices of American cheese. Later in life, when my cat Dada died, I ate an entire 11 by 9-inch pan of broccoli cheese casserole in a single sitting.

When I lost my appetite, I got scared. Because it wasn't just that I wasn't hungry. It was that I *couldn't* eat. The week after we officially split, I sat at my desk at work—it was ridiculous that I was at work, but I had to be *somewhere*—and I gagged on a spoonful of oatmeal. I grabbed the wastebasket under my desk, and when nothing happened I ran quickly to a single stall bathroom and lay on the floor. My body was rejecting everything but water, and I'd never felt so fully that I'd lost my footing, that life wasn't worth living, that everything was wrong.

A couple months later, I went back to Puerto Rico seeking restoration, renewal, and a way back to myself. Because the island was mine. You'll often hear Puerto Ricans describe the island as if we each individually own it. *Mi islita bonita—my* beautiful island. I felt that ownership. I needed to be with her. Despite all the childhood angst I'd felt, somewhere along the way the island had become my sanctuary.

The first day on the island, I had dinner with friends at the Casita Miramar—an upscale Puerto Rican restaurant that prepares fancied-up traditional dishes. Even their *tostones* are lovely, delicate, and airy. But nothing was appetizing.

For months I'd been eating a very limited diet—oatmeal, smoothies, chicken breasts, and baby spinach. Whenever I deviated, I felt awful. I settled on an avocado stuffed with octopus in coconut sauce. It was exquisite and delicate, the octopus bringing out the sweetness of the avocado's flesh, the sauce accentuating its vegetal fattiness. I ate half of it, slowly and intentionally. It was a start.

But that night I woke up in a cold sweat from a recurring nightmare. My ex-husband told me he'd be better. And I believed him, let him back in . . . and then there was the crushing realization: he'd lied to me again. Once awake, I couldn't get back to sleep. I stepped out on the balcony and breathed in the salty air, watching the palm trees bend and shake in the breeze.

I waited until the sun came up, made myself a strong cup of coffee with lots of brown sugar, and started another day of something like starvation.

The emptiness I felt in my body was immense, a black hole that nothing could fill. Everything reminded me of him because he was with me the last time I was there. And the time before that, Tata was still alive.

As the days passed, I began introducing little bits of food. One thing I could bear to eat was *pan sobao*. White bread baked into loaves, pillowy soft with a slightly chewy sweetish crust, and like any bread best eaten hot and fresh from the oven. Often in the security line at San Juan Airport you'll see people with loaves of *pan sobao* peeking out of their carry-on bags. I bought a daily loaf and would munch on it, golf ball–sized chunks at a time, nibbling like a mouse.

Fresh mango and pineapple were also good, as were small amounts of *pinchos de pollo* (grilled chicken skewers) and juice; fresh dried coconut, ivory pieces with the soft brown skin still attached that you could chew and chew and chew. At some farmers'

markets I found vegan baked goods and gluten-free *guanabana* and almond cake. My taste buds were so delicate that I really enjoyed these mild flavors. I'd always associated Puerto Rican food with fat, oil, pork, and knock-you-out heaviness, but everywhere I went I gratefully found something light and nourishing.

Each day I discovered new foods on the island that helped me nurse myself back to health emotionally and physically. At the end of my stay on the island, I made time to visit my friend Cruz, who took me to his friend's restaurant in Yabucoa, a small mountainous rain forest with giant boulders stacked on top of each other forming uncanny sculptures called Las Piedras (the rocks). They line the sides of the narrow mountain roads with concrete houses and steep stone stairs nestled between them. There, Sabor Boricua—possibly the most generic name for a Puerto Rican restaurant—sits on a ridge overlooking a wild jungle farm of yucca, plantain, and breadfruit.

I knew as soon as I arrived that this was the restaurant of my dreams. A handful of round tables sat to the right of the bar, a rectangular one to the left. On the far end, a giant cast-iron pot sat atop a wood fire. There was a bubbling cauldron brimming with *ternera en fricassee* (braised veal), bobbing in a broth with *sofrito,* wine, beer, brandy, *calabaza* (pumpkin), and potatoes.

We sat at the tiny bar, just a few stools and enough space for four elbows, and met the chef, Berto, a tall, round-bellied man with a smile that could stop traffic. All teeth and mischievous eyes and decades of crow's

feet and laugh lines around his eyes and mouth.

Berto overheard me talking about my sadness and hunger, and his face softened with understanding. He poured me a *chichaito de tamarindo*, a shot made of *pitorro* (sugar cane moonshine) infused with tamarind.

"*Bueno m'ija—hoy si que vas a comer!*" he said, that big smile returning to his face. Girl, today you're going to eat!

And I did eat. I ate and I ate and I ate. Berto kept close watch, bringing out plates piled high every hour or so, along with fresh drinks—whiskey with coconut water. First he brought out a plate of *carne frita*—chunks of boneless pork ribs marinated in *adobo* then deep-fried, served with toothpicks. Then *tostones* and *pique* (green plantains fried then smashed with hot sauce).

Slowly I felt myself come back to life in this magical mountain kitchen. I walked up to the bubbling cauldron and asked questions. I stirred, I tasted.

Berto invited me into his tiny indoor kitchen attached to the bar. It reminded me of my kitchen in New York, and was like my grandmother's kitchen. Just barely enough room for two people to stand, one small basic gas stove, pots hanging from walls, every surface covered with something about to be cooked. He was making *arroz con tocino* (white rice with crisped pork fat) and *petit pois con patitas de cerdo* (green peas with pig's feet).

"*El secreto es dejarlo sin tocar, y moverlo solo una vez—al momento perfecto,*" he said, describing the rice. The secret is not to touch it, and then stir it at the exact right moment.

On that mountaintop, surrounded by friendly strangers who loved food as much as I did and treated me as if they'd known me my whole life . . . I was happy in a way I'd never been before. I didn't know it until I got there, but what I'd understood as a kind of forced starvation was more like a cleanse. My body knew better than me that I needed to fast, to recalibrate, to come to terms with the pain. It was a pain deepened by its connection to the experience of watching my mother struggle after my parents got divorced. Deepened through a new understanding of the pain my grandmother experienced when her husband left.

We arrived at Sabor Boricua at noon and left at 8 p.m. I ate so much and drank so many *chichaitos* and whiskey and coconut waters that I nearly left my purse at the restaurant. Berto gave me a container full of food in case I was hungry when I got home. I was beyond content.

Still, I cried myself to sleep that night as I had so many others. It was just the beginning of healing, of reconnecting, of making a new home for myself on the island. On my own, untethered.

I'd been brought to a boil and simmered slow, then stirred at exactly the right moment.

Six months later, I again traveled back to Puerto Rico, which I now need to do at regular intervals. In stark contrast to the mixed feeling of dread, apprehension, and curiosity I had as a child, I felt only joy, excitement, and a deep sense that I belonged there.

I knew my way around. And not just what streets to drive down, but also the best *panaderías*, what time of year to find the ripest *quenepas*, where the perfect remote beaches are, and exactly what insult to yell at someone when they drive their car in reverse down the exit ramp on the interstate. (*Animal! Coño, que te pasa?!*)

I went with Cybelle Codish—the photographer for this book—who had never been before. We barely knew each other but immediately fell into a rhythm. I enjoyed being a guide, knowing that I could show her things she wouldn't otherwise see.

We returned to Berto's restaurant in Yabucoa, twice. Once just to eat, drink, and dance. And then again so I could cook with Berto and learn how to make one of my favorite dishes: *conejo estofado* (braised rabbit). It was a beautiful day, sunny, not too hot, the breeze coming through at just the right moment, chickens and stray dogs visiting and scavenging. I was there all day, again, and met his entire family and extended community: neighbors and local elected officials. His son made us appetizers, and his wife made it her mission to teach me how to dance salsa properly.

"Entras y sales como las holas del mar," she said. You come and go like the ocean's waves.

As the hours passed, I'd laughed so hard and often my stomach muscles ached, and I felt so right with the world. Berto took me under his wing, teaching me how to prepare some of his favorite dishes, step by step, just like Tata. I felt her all around me; she and my mother. This restaurant was not a restaurant but a big, open dining room, inviting and welcoming. Its purpose was only partly to serve food. More so, it served to bring folks together to enjoy a beer or a meal, to make a friend, to lend an ear or get advice; to find someone to play dominoes with or a pretty girl to dance with. It was as if my grandmother's *marquesina* had been moved to the mountains.

On my last night on the island, Cybelle and I went to the beach by moonlight, a bottle of rum tucked under my arm to toast the end of our travels. It was hurricane season, and the forecast warned us ahead of time that it was supposed to thunderstorm every day of our trip. But it never rained, until it did.

As we stood at the edge of the ocean, the sky opened up suddenly and showered us with fat, violent rain, the wind whipping around us, the waves crashing against our shins trying hard to pull us in. After an immeasurable amount of time, the sky cleared as quickly as it had darkened. We were left standing there, shivering, looking at each other, exuberant but puzzled, not fully understanding what had happened.

But the *bruja* in me knew that I'd been visited by Tata, by Yemaya, by Mami, by Oya. That the five of us had come into alignment somewhere among the mountains, the rain forest, the oceans, as well as the *sancocho*, the *conejo estofado*, the fresh coconuts, and *bacalaítos*.

And I knew I'd finally found my place on the island. That it was now my home again.

RECIPES

While much of my return to the island was painful at first, it also opened my eyes to new ways of preparing healthy, vegetable-forward Puerto Rican food. The recipes in this chapter are largely vegetarian (many vegan) and seafood recipes. Ultimately, they better reflect the way I eat today, and the untapped potential for Puerto Rican food to be nourishing, healthy, and light.

Camarones Empanizados de Plátano (Plantain-Crusted Shrimp)

Mango Remoulade

Ceviche Peru-Puerto

Ensalada de Berro con China y Aguacate (Watercress Salad with Orange and Avocado)

Una Majada (Mashed Root Vegetables)

Chayotes Rellenos (Chayote Squash Stuffed with Picadillo)

Ensalada de Chayote y Habichuelas Tiernas (Chayote and Green Bean Salad)

Broccoli, Scallion, and Coconut Milk Puree

Sopa de Caupí, Arroz, y Leche de Coco (Cowpea, Rice, and Coconut Milk Stew)

Gandules con Bolitas de Plátano (Pigeon Peas with Plantain Dumplings)

Tembleque (Coconut Panna Cotta)

Mundo Nuevo (Fresh Corn Coconut Pudding)

Más Que un Mojito (More Than a Mojito)

Camarones Empanizados de Plátano (Plantain-Crusted Shrimp)

Mariquitas, or plantain chips, are an everyday snack in Puerto Rico, but you can also increasingly find them in stores here on the U.S. mainland. Crushed up, they make a great breading for flash-fried shrimp.

Serves 6 as appetizer

1½ pounds large shrimp

1 (2.5-ounce) bag plantain chips

1 cup panko bread crumbs

1 teaspoon garlic powder

½ teaspoon paprika

¼ teaspoon salt

¼ teaspoon ground black pepper

⅛ teaspoon cayenne pepper

3 large egg whites

Mango Remoulade (page 140)

Mayo-Ketchup (page 68) or Salsa de Aguacate (page 101)

Peel and devein the shrimp, leaving the tails attached.

In a food processor, grind the plantain chips into fine crumbs. Pour the crumbs into a large bowl. Mix in the bread crumbs, garlic powder, paprika, salt, black pepper, and cayenne. Stir with a fork to incorporate, then pour onto a large plate.

In a deep bowl, whisk the egg whites with a fork for about 1 minute, until frothy.

Set up an assembly line in this order: shrimp on the left, then egg whites, plantain bread crumbs, and a wire rack set on a large cookie sheet. Dredge the shrimp in egg white, then dip in bread crumbs, using your other hand to pour bread crumbs evenly over both sides, and then set on the rack.

Preheat the broiler to high. Place the sheet directly under the broiler and broil for 5 to 7 minutes, flipping halfway through, until the shrimp are cooked through and browned all over. Remove from the broiler and let sit for a minute. Serve with mango remoulade and mayo-ketchup or creamy avocado sauce.

Ceviche Peru-Puerto

The first time I had ceviche was when I was in my twenties at a Peruvian restaurant on Buford Highway, a now famous stretch of highway outside of Atlanta that's fabulously international. I instantly fell in love with the sweetness of the yams and the corn, the citrusy tartness, and fresh tender fish. I could eat it all day, every day. Here's my take, made Puerto Rican by my hand and a little culantro.

Serves 6

1¼ pounds boneless, skinless white fish fillets (red snapper, flounder, or sole), cut into 1-inch pieces

1 large sweet potato, peeled and cut into 1-inch cubes

½ red onion, thinly sliced

3 *ají dulce* chiles, ribs and seeds removed and thinly sliced

1 garlic clove

¼ cup fresh lime juice

¼ cup fresh lemon juice

1½ teaspoons salt

1 teaspoon finely chopped fresh cilantro

1 tablespoon finely chopped fresh culantro

2 cups fresh corn kernels, cut from the cob

Freshly ground black pepper

Rinse the fish in cold water, then dry well with paper towels.

Set a steamer basket over a saucepan of simmering water, making sure the bottom of the basket doesn't touch the water. Add the sweet potatoes and steam for 7 minutes, or until tender. Run the sweet potatoes under cold water, then drain and set aside.

Combine the red onion, chiles, garlic, lime juice, lemon juice, salt, cilantro, and culantro and mix well. Add the fish and gently toss to incorporate. Let marinate for 10 minutes.

Add the sweet potatoes and raw corn and toss again. Taste and season with more salt if needed and some pepper. Let chill at least 1 hour in the fridge, then serve.

Note: **Fish for ceviche should always be fresh, not frozen.**

Ensalada de Berro con China y Aguacate (Watercress Salad with Orange and Avocado)

When I started cooking my way through Tata's 1964 copy of *Cocina Criolla*, I was surprised to find a number of recipes including watercress. Having only ever eaten it sautéed in Chinese dishes, simmered in soups, or on sandwiches and in salads, I'm still not sure how it made its way into this Puerto Rican classic. Here's my contribution and homage to this green and Carmen Aboy Valldejuli—author of *Cocina Criolla*—and her inventive cooking.

Serves 4

Dressing

1 tablespoon fresh lime juice

1 tablespoon fresh orange juice

2 tablespoons olive oil

¼ teaspoon Dijon mustard

Salt and freshly ground black pepper to taste

Salad

2 large bunches watercress

1 small orange

2 small ripe avocados, peeled and pits removed

½ cup walnuts, toasted

Freshly ground black pepper

Make the dressing: Combine all the dressing ingredients and whisk with a fork until full incorporated and slightly thickened.

Make the salad: Fill a bowl with cold water and swish the watercress in the water to rinse it. Drain well. Cut the watercress, stems included, into 1-inch pieces and put them in a large bowl. Supreme the orange (cut off all the peel and the surrounding membrane of each segment), then cut the orange segments into ½-inch pieces, discarding the seeds and adding the pieces to the bowl with the watercress. Cut the avocados into ½-inch pieces and add them to the bowl.

Pour the dressing over the salad and toss well. Sprinkle with the toasted walnuts and finish with some black pepper. Serve immediately.

Mango Remoulade

Makes about 1 cup

½ large ripe mango, finely diced

1 tablespoon minced scallion

1 garlic clove, minced

½ cup mayonnaise

½ teaspoon fresh lime juice

Dash of hot sauce

Salt and freshly ground black pepper to taste

Combine all the ingredients in a medium bowl and mix well. Refrigerate before serving.

Una Majada
(Mashed Root Vegetables)

One of the cornerstones of Puerto Rican food is root vegetables, and their variety and flavor can be mysterious to outsiders. They come in various shapes, sizes, and funky—sometimes hairy—peels. But each has a distinct flavor. Here's my take on something better than mashed potatoes, which are increasingly being served on the island.

Serves 4 as a side

1½ tablespoons salt, plus more to taste

3 cups peeled and chopped yautía

4 cups peeled and chopped ñame

2½ cups peeled and chopped yucca

4 tablespoons (¼ cup) unsalted butter

Freshly ground black pepper

Bring 4 quarts of water to a boil in a large stockpot and add the salt. Add the yautía, ñame, and yucca and boil for 30 minutes, or until root vegetables are slightly translucent and are pierced easily with a knife.

Drain, reserving ½ cup of the cooking water. Transfer the roots to a large bowl. Add the butter and the reserved cooking water and mash with a potato masher until smooth. Season with salt and pepper and serve.

Chayotes Rellenos (Chayote Squash Stuffed with Picadillo)

It wasn't until 2011 that I saw my first chayote, at a Mexican grocery store in East Harlem, so I was surprised to find out about all the ways folks in Puerto Rico eat them. This is a simple weeknight meal that can easily be made vegetarian with a meat substitute such as seitan, tofu, or beans for the *picadillo*.

Serves 4

2 tablespoons salt

4 large chayotes

Vegetable oil cooking spray

1 cup Picadillo (page 36)

2 tablespoons crumbled feta cheese

In a large saucepan, bring 2 quarts of water to a boil over high heat. Add the salt. While the water is coming up to a boil, prepare a large bowl of ice water.

Cut the chayotes in half and remove the seed from the center. Add them to the pot one by one, reduce the heat to medium, and cook for 25 minutes, or until the chayotes are easily pierced with a knife.

Carefully remove the chayotes from the pan one half at a time, place them in the ice water to cool, then drain and pat them dry with a paper towel.

While the chayotes are boiling, preheat the oven to 375°F. Spray a rimmed baking sheet with cooking spray.

Scoop a layer of flesh from each chayote—about half, so that the shells retain their shape—and put the flesh in a large bowl. Arrange the chayotes cut-side up on the prepared baking sheet.

Mash the reserved chayote flesh and fold in the picadillo and feta cheese until well combined and the mixture holds together well. Carefully scoop into the hollowed-out chayotes.

Place in the center rack of the oven and bake for 10 to 15 minutes, until heated through and the top is browned. Remove from the oven and serve.

Broccoli, Scallion, and Coconut Milk Puree

The first cookbook I became obsessed with was Deborah Madison's *Vegetarian Cooking for Everyone*. Over the years I've cooked at least a hundred recipes from it, and it continues to be my go-to vegetable encyclopedia. This recipe is adapted from one of my favorite recipes in that book. Serve as a side or add vegetable stock to turn it into a pureed soup.

Serves 4 as a side

1 (13.5-ounce) can coconut milk, or 1½ cups fresh coconut milk (page 15)

2 large bunches broccoli (including stems), chopped

6 scallions, white and green parts, chopped

½ teaspoon salt

Cracked black pepper

In a large saucepan, bring the coconut milk to a simmer over medium heat.

Add the broccoli and scallions, return to a simmer, and simmer, uncovered, for 5 minutes. Remove from the heat and use an immersion blender to blend into a loose puree. Add the salt, season with pepper, and serve.

Ensalada de Chayote y Habichuelas Tiernas (Chayote and Green Bean Salad)

Green beans are among the most commonly eaten vegetables in classic Puerto Rican food, but too often they're canned or frozen. Here's a simple, fresh, crisp salad that's a great starter, particularly for a heavy meal.

Serves 6 as a side or starter

2 tablespoons kosher salt, plus more to taste

1 pound fresh green beans, tipped and cut into 2-inch sections

1 pound chayote squash, cut into 1-inch cubes

1 pound tomatoes, coarsely chopped

2 tablespoons olive oil

1 tablespoon fresh lemon juice

½ teaspoon lemon zest

Freshly ground black pepper

Prepare an ice bath by emptying a tray of ice cubes into a large bowl and adding the 2 tablespoons salt and enough water to cover. Set aside.

Bring a large saucepan of water to a boil over high heat and salt the water. Add the green beans and cook until crisp-tender, about 2 minutes. Remove from the pan, transfer to the ice bath to cool, then drain. Add the chayote to the boiling water and cook until crisp-tender, about 2 minutes. Drain and transfer to the ice bath to cool, then drain again.

In a large bowl, combine the green beans, chayote, tomatoes, oil, lemon juice, and lemon zest. Season with salt and pepper and serve.

Sopa de Caupí, Arroz, y Leche de Coco (Cowpea, Rice, and Coconut Milk Stew)

This dish is adapted from *Cocine a Gusto*, another one of the classic Puerto Rican cookbooks I inherited from Tata. It's a take on Jamaican rice and peas, and the cowpeas have an almost peanut-y flavor that makes this a really earthy and satisfying vegan dish.

Serves 8

1 tablespoon olive oil

1 large onion, finely chopped

2 garlic cloves, minced

1 (14-ounce) can diced tomatoes

6 fresh culantro leaves, finely chopped

2 bay leaves

5 cups Vegetable Stock (page 13)

3 cups fresh coconut milk (page 15) or 2 (13.5-ounce) cans coconut milk

1 pound dried cowpeas, soaked overnight in water to cover by a few inches and drained

2 cups basmati rice, rinsed and soaked in water to cover for 10 minutes and drained

Heat the oil in a large, heavy-bottomed saucepan over medium-high heat. Add onion and cook for 3 minutes, or until softened and starting to color. Add the garlic and cook for 30 seconds, or until fragrant.

Add the tomatoes, culantro, and bay leaves and bring to a simmer.

Add the stock, 1 cup of the coconut milk, and the drained cowpeas and bring to a boil. Reduce the heat to medium-low, cover, and simmer for 10 minutes, or until the cowpeas are just about tender.

Add the drained rice to the cooked cowpeas in broth along with the remaining 2 cups coconut milk. Bring back to a boil, then reduce the heat to low, cover, and simmer for 10 more minutes, or until the rice and cowpeas are fully cooked but not mushy. Use more water for a soupier dish or less stock for a firmer rice and peas dish.

Gandules con Bolitas de Plátano (Pigeon Peas with Plantain Dumplings)

Every time I ask my mother what she wants me to cook, it's this homey and incredibly nourishing vegan dish. The recipe can be adjusted in any number of ways—more spice in the plantain balls, more seasoning in the *gandules*. Add fresh spinach or a poached egg to change up leftovers.

Serves 8

Gandules

1 tablespoon olive oil

¾ cup Sofrito (page 10)

8 cups Vegetable Stock (page 13)

2 bay leaves

1 teaspoon salt, plus more to taste

Freshly ground black pepper

1½ pounds frozen *gandules* (pigeon peas)

Plantain Balls

3 green plantains (see Note), peeled and soaked in water to cover until ready to use

1 teaspoon ground cumin

½ teaspoon ground *achiote* or sweet paprika

1 teaspoon garlic powder

1½ teaspoons salt

Garnishes: fresh chopped cilantro, culantro, avocado, and/or tomato

Make the *gandules*: Heat the oil in a large saucepan over medium-high heat. Add the sofrito and cook for about 7 minutes, until the mixture starts to brown and the liquid is mostly evaporated. Add the stock, bay leaves, salt, pepper to taste, and the *gandules* and bring to a boil. Lower the heat and simmer for about 15 minutes, until the *gandules* are fully tender but not falling apart.

While the *gandules* are cooking, make the plantain balls: Grate the plantains in a food processor fitted with the grating blade or on the coarse holes of a box grater. Put the grated plantains in a large bowl, add the cumin, achiote, garlic powder, and salt and mix well.

Roll about 1 tablespoon of the plantain mixture between your hands into balls. The starch from the plantains will keep them from sticking to your hands. Set the plantain balls on a large plate with a little space between them. Refrigerate until you are ready to cook them.

After the *gandules* have cooked for 15 minutes, add the plantain balls one by one and bring back to a boil. Lower the heat and cook for 2 more minutes, or until the plantain balls are firm but still tender. Season with salt and pepper and remove from the heat. Spoon into bowls and add your choice of garnishes.

Note: The plantains should be very green. If they are even close to yellow, they won't stick together.

Tembleque
(Coconut Panna Cotta)

Tembleque is a common Puerto Rican dessert with a wonderful name that refers to its trembling, wiggly texture, like panna cotta or flan mixed with Jell-O.

When I would visit Tata as a kid, she often bought *tembleque* from her favorite bakery in Bayamon. It always came in a round aluminum container with a clear plastic lid, revealing its sprinkled cinnamon topping. I would open it, breathe in the coconut-y cinnamon aroma, and we would sit on her *marquesina* and eat it out of the container with a spoon.

Tembleque has six ingredients, only one of which—orange flower water—is a little obscure. You should be able to find it at your local *botánica* or stores specializing in Middle Eastern ingredients. It's not essential, but it adds a signature flavor that's worth the search.

Serves 10

½ cup cornstarch

⅔ cup sugar (or ½ cup if using canned coconut milk)

½ teaspoon salt

1 teaspoon orange flower water (*agua de azahar*)

4 cups coconut milk, fresh (page 15) or canned

Ground cinnamon

In a large saucepan, combine the cornstarch, sugar, salt, and orange flower water. Slowly whisk in the coconut milk until well incorporated.

Heat over medium-high heat, stirring continuously with a wooden spoon, until the mixture starts to thicken. Lower the heat to medium and continue stirring until just barely boiling. Remove from the heat and immediately pour into a 9-inch-diameter, 3-inch-deep mold of any shape, using a rubber scraper to get at any tembleque from the sides of the pot (alternatively, pour it into individual molds).

Allow to cool fully, about 1 hour, then cover and refrigerate until cold, at least 4 hours.

Flip the *tembleque* onto a plate and sprinkle with cinnamon, or scoop right out of the mold and serve.

Note: I strongly recommend fresh coconut milk, but canned works well too, with a slight adjustment on the amount of sugar.

Mundo Nuevo
(Fresh Corn Coconut Pudding)

This classic recipe is no longer commonly found on the island, but it has a remarkable flavor profile and is well worth making. Special thanks to chef and friend Ben Mims for helping adapt this recipe.

Serves 6 to 8

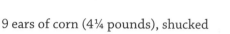

9 ears of corn (4¼ pounds), shucked

2 cups coconut milk, fresh (page 15) or canned

1 cup sugar (or ¾ cup if using canned coconut milk)

1¼ teaspoons kosher salt

1 star anise pod

Cut the kernels from the ears of corn and transfer to a blender (you should have 5½ to 6 cups kernels). Using the back of a knife and working over the blender, scrape along the spent cobs to remove any "milk" from them, letting it drain into the blender. Add the coconut milk, sugar, and salt and blend until smooth, about 1 minute.

Pour the corn liquid through a fine-mesh sieve set over a large saucepan; scrape and press on the solids until no more liquid remains. Discard the solids. Add the star anise and place the pan over high heat. Cook, whisking often, until the mixture begins to boil, then continue to cook for about 1 minute more, until it thickens.

Pour the corn liquid into an 8-inch square or 9-inch round serving dish (or 8 small pudding cups or ramekins), discard the star anise pod, and cool to room temperature. Refrigerate the custard for at least 2 hours, until set, or overnight before serving.

Más Que Un Mojito (More Than a Mojito)

In 2014, I hosted a supper club with my good friends Marisa Cadena and Ken Ho at their restaurant, Lucky Luna. Marisa invented this incredible cocktail, a take on a classic mojito incorporating culantro instead of mint and using pineapple and vanilla. It's refreshing, complex, and addictive.

Makes 1 cocktail

1 teaspoon turbinado sugar

¾ lime, sliced

2 fresh culantro leaves, plus additional for garnish

1 to 2 small drops vanilla extract

1 ounce pineapple juice

2 ounces rum

Club soda

In a deep glass, muddle the sugar, lime, and culantro until the sugar is mostly dissolved. Add the vanilla, pineapple juice, and rum and stir.

Add ice to cover the mixture, then top with soda water. Garnish with a whole culantro leaf.

Acknowledgments

"A mal tiempo, buena cara." *In bad times, put on a happy face.*

At the time of this writing, the majority of Puerto Ricans still on the island are without power. Telecommunications have been down, gasoline has been sparse, and contaminated water sources are the only option for many people.

On September 20, 2017, Hurricane María made landfall on the southeast corner of Puerto Rico. I haven't been able to communicate reliably with my people, like so many others with family on the island. I know they're alive, but I've only received sporadic messages that mostly say "Estamos bien." *We're okay*. Not long ago, after weeks of not hearing from her, Mami received a voicemail from my cousin, Bianca.

"Estamos bien. Gracias a dios no nos paso mucho, más que unas matas de plátano caídas." *We're fine. Thank God we didn't lose too much, just a few downed plantain trees.*

Based on the constellation of news reports, one thing is certain—my people are suffering. Houses missing roofs, El Yunque rainforest looking like a pile of match sticks, lush hillsides turned to hay. And I can't help but wonder what people are eating. I've seen reports of stripped-down grocery stores, and food recovery packages from FEMA and other agencies with nonperishables ranging from canned meats to Cheez-Its.

I suppose it's a mixed blessing that Puerto Ricans are used to crisis-eating. Cooking with processed foods, and making a meal of a pile of rice, a fried egg, and ketchup are arguably among the most authentically Puerto

Rican ways of eating. I've heard that macaroni and cheese with Spam is a post-María favorite.

But I've been haunted by a text message I received from my friend Cruz, which he sent as María made landfall.

"DEVASTADOR . . . INFERNO . . . !!! LA ISLA TIRARA PA'LANTE PERO NECESITARÁ MAS DE 6 MESES. AÚN SOPLA SIN PIEDAD EN GURABO." *Devastating. This is hell. The island will rise up, but we'll need more than 6 months. The winds are mercilessly blowing in Gurabo.*

It's the word "devastador" that I can't get out of my head. There is no better word. The last storm of this magnitude hit Puerto Rico in 1932; before mass transit, before electricity and running water were widespread, before the internet. There's no modern precedent for this level of destruction. And it's difficult to imagine how we'll rebuild.

Many of my friends and colleagues with Puerto Rican roots here on the mainland are, like me, keeping a close watch on how things unfold. I'm planning to return as soon as I can catch a plane. With so much need it's difficult to know how to respond, but if I go perhaps I can put my feet deep in the earth and listen to the trees whisper; perhaps the island will tell me what she needs from me now.

There are a lot of people there I need to see. Like my friend Berto, whose restaurant and mischievous, twinkling eyes brought me back from the brink. He and his family live in Yabucoa—the city where María's eye struck. I've heard very little from him, save a text message.

"Hola, estamos bien ante todo." *Hi, we're good despite it all.*

Things will (hopefully) be better in coming months. The power will be back across the island. The roads will be clear, water will be clean, and folks will be pulling their lives back together. Or, they will be migrating to the mainland . . . likely in droves. That journey has already begun for many.

As I reviewed the contents of this book once more, I've relived my journey to reconnect with the beautiful, soulful place where I was born but had felt estranged from for so long. The island, so seductive and intoxicating, nourishing me with its food, its salty sea air, its rain forests and the generous, boisterous laughter of its people. And I'm amazed by how beautifully Cybelle Codish, the photographer for this book, documented the lusciousness of the island. But many of the places she captured don't exist anymore; at least, not in the same way.

As Tata used to say, "A mal tiempo, buena cara." *In bad times, put on a happy face.* I've heard terrible things, but I've also heard stories of people on the island doing everything in their power to overcome, to help each other. Little leaves are growing back on bare trees, people are charging electronics in their cars while they help deliver goods to people in need. My good friend and mentor, Carolina González, recently shared with me the story of a rural town where residents are refusing to leave, despite nearly total destruction, because they need to protect the local bees. "Who else will put out sugar water so the *abejas* can continue to do their work?" they ask.

Pa'lante—moving forward. *Despacito*—in due time. We'll call on the Taíno god, Yukiyú, to rebuild El Yunque branch by branch, sprout new plantain groves, and fertile grasslands for animals to graze. We're entering a new chapter in the history of *la isla*. May we do so by acknowledging the shortcomings and political machinations that have brought so much suffering to the island and its people, as well as the potential of this metamorphosis.

Every word, every recipe, every image in this book was made possible by my generous, brilliant, and loving community. I owe so much to so many people, but I want to acknowledge a handful in particular who are in my heart and in this book's pages.

Gracias to my many teachers, because school was my sanctuary during the tough times. To Mrs. Richardson, my kindergarten teacher, who let me spend as much time as I wanted to flipping through books I could not yet read. To Mrs. Scruggs, my middle school orchestra conductor, who taught me to stand up to bullies. To Mrs. Linda Boot, my high school social studies teacher, who showed me that the history I had been taught was biased and flawed. To Dr. Elizabeth Hackett, my college advisor, who gave me my first feminist education and changed my life. And to Ada Ferrer, my grad school advisor, who gave me the opportunity to become a storyteller and trained me to be a careful oral historian.

In addition to schoolteachers, I am fortunate to have a mighty team of mentors who guide and inspire me. To Carolina González, who took a chance on my earliest radio work and continues to advise me on my career, my cooking, and my heart. To Yvonne Latty, for being such a fierce example of a Caribbean woman, a survivor, a mother, a journalist, and a friend; you've given me a lot to live up to. To Martina Guzmán, for inspiring me, believing in me, and for your boundless sisterhood.

To Kathy Gunst, for putting me in the direct path of so much success and lifting me up during my darkest moments. And to John Rudolph, for making me a journalist and taking a chance on the very first words that would become this book. Kathy, John, you are my family.

A very special thanks to my agent, Lisa Ekus, and the inimitable Sally Ekus, for taking a chance on this project and helping me bring it home. To my editor, Sian Hunter, at the University Press of Florida, and copyeditor, Leda Scheintaub, for making my stories sing. And to the rest of the team at the University Press of Florida, thank you for working hard to bring new voices to the culinary world.

To Cybelle Codish, who is so much more than the photographer of this book. You are a magic woman, and your infectious energy and incredible artistry make everything beautiful. I can't wait for our next adventure.

Good cooks need good eaters, and I'm grateful to everyone who has eaten at my table, chopped onions with me, taught me new skills, and grown my community of fellow food folks. To Jenny Williams, with whom I've hosted countless dinner parties, held hands over gin and tonics, and who cemented my love for vegetables. To my favorite sous chefs, Kris Mordecai and Arianna Bennett, who braved beef tongue and *pavochón*, and have tasted nearly everything in this book. To my road dog Stephanie

Rodriguez, for shopping, chopping, tasting, styling, and deejaying dozens of parties with me. To Lisa Thrower: I often think about that salade niçoise, making cassoulet, and lying on the floor while you were pregnant with IV. To Marisa Cadena, for showing up on a snowy day with sparkling wine and chocolate to help dry my tears, for teaching me to open a bottle of wine with the heel of a boot; and her partner Ken Ho for co-hosting my first supper club.

I've lived a lot of places, each of which holds a piece of my heart. To my Atlanta crew, who were my first taste teachers: Christian Vick, Jenna Novick, Keely Harris. My Bay Area crew: Nathalie Wade, Jen Bloomer, Laura Brennan Bissell, Fiona Ruddy. My NYC crew: Nadia Reiman, Natalia Fidelholtz, Carolina Ramirez, Roque Planas, Alletta Cooper, Liyna Anwar, Emily Martinez, Jud Esty-Kendall, Leigh and Charlie Thompson-Shealy. My PR crew: Cruz Ortiz Cuadra and Berto.

Finally, to my family, to whom this book is dedicated. Tata, espero que siempre estés orgullosa de mi, donde sea que estas. Mami, Kristina, you are my world. Itege (Bianquita cuando eramos niñas), I'm so lucky to have you back in my life and to learn from you. Tio Julin, Titi Eblis, Titi Sarita, y mis primos—los quiero tanto. Papi, for being the first person to trust me with a skillet, and teaching me to make pancakes. And Sarah, my sister from another mister. I could write hundreds of pages about all we've shared, and even more about where I imagine we'll go together; 'til the wheels fall off.

Index

WHEN HER FAMILY MOVED from Puerto Rico to Atlanta, Von Diaz traded plantains, roast pork, and malta for grits, fried chicken, and sweet tea. Brimming with humor and nostalgia, *Coconuts and Collards* is a recipe-packed memoir of growing up Latina in the Deep South.

The stories center on the women in Diaz's family who have used food to nourish and care for one another. When her mother—newly single and with two young daughters—took a second job to make ends meet, Diaz taught herself to cook, preparing meals for her sister after school, feeding her mother when she came home late from work. During summer visits to Puerto Rico, her grandmother guided her rediscovery of the island's flavors and showed her traditional cooking techniques. Years later the island called her back to its warm and tropical embrace to be comforted by its familiar flavors.

Inspired by her grandmother's 1962 copy of *Cocina Criolla*—the Puerto Rican equivalent of the *Joy of Cooking*—*Coconuts and Collards* celebrates traditional recipes while fusing them with Diaz's own family history and a contemporary Southern flair. Diaz discovers the connections between the food she grew up eating in Atlanta and the African and indigenous influences in so many Puerto Rican dishes. The *funche* recipe is grits kicked up with coconut milk. White beans make the catfish corn chowder creamy and give it a Spanish feel. The *pinchos de pollo*—chicken skewers—feature guava BBQ sauce, which doubles as the sauce for *adobo*-coated ribs. The *pastelón* is shepherd's pie . . . with sweet plantains. And the *quingombo* recipe would be recognized as stewed okra in any Southern kitchen, even if it is laced with warm and aromatic *sofrito*.

Diaz innovates for modern palates, updating and lightening recipes and offering vegetarian alternatives. For the *chayotes rellenos* (stuffed squash), she suggests replacing the *picadillo* (sautéed ground beef) with seitan or tofu. She offers alternatives for difficult-to-find ingredients, like substituting potatoes for *yucca* and *yautía*—root vegetables typically paired with a meat to make *sancocho*. Diaz's version of this hearty stew features chicken and lean pork.

And because every good Puerto Rican meal ends with drinks, desserts, and dancing, Diaz includes recipes for *besitos de coco* (coconut kisses), rum cake, *sofrito* bloody marys, and *anticuado*, an old-fashioned made with rum.

With stunning photographs that showcase the geographic diversity of the island and the vibrant ingredients that make up Puerto Rican cuisine, this cookbook is a moving story about discovering our roots through the foods that comfort us. It is about the foods that remind us of family and help us bridge childhood and adulthood, island and mainland, birthplace and adopted home.